About the au

Peter Frank was born in North Wales and grew up in North West England. Educationally he was an under-achiever — he scraped into grammar school, where between the ages of sixteen and eighteen he failed all his A-Levels and, notably, failed the English Language O-Level examination six times. He started work as a bonus clerk and then moved on to become a computer operator. Later, his work involved running acceptance tests on mainframe computers — allowing him to travel widely in Britain, Czechoslovakia, and Russia. He then went to Australia for two years, where he began his career in computer sales. He ended his career as a Vice President of Software Sales, before moving to Austria for love. He graduated with a 2:1 BA Honours degree in European Studies in 2008.

GROWING UP WITH FOREIGNERS

Peter Frank

GROWING UP WITH FOREIGNERS

Vanguard Press

VANGUARD PAPERBACK

A CIP catalogue record for this title is
available from the British Library.

ISBN 978 1 78465 726 0

*Vanguard Press is an imprint of
Pegasus Elliot MacKenzie Publishers Ltd.*
www.pegasuspublishers.com

First Published in 2020

**Vanguard Press
Sheraton House Castle Park
Cambridge England**

Printed & Bound in Great Britain

Dedication

This book is dedicated to my grandparents, Ilona and Edmund Frank and Bianca and Adolf Blaschke; my parents, Christine and Henry Frank; my father's cousin, Evy von Seemann, and her half-cousin, Marietta (Ditte) von Puscariu; my aunt, Waldtraut Hagel, and her husband Jupp Hagel; my sister Helen Rockman (née Frank); and my cousins Hildegard Staudinger (née Hagel) and Karl Heinz Hagel (all deceased). In addition, it is dedicated to my cousin, Brigitte Fuchs-Bodde (née Hagel), and to my wife Ellie, my son Matthew and my daughter Vanessa.

Acknowledgements

This book could not have been written without my grandparents and my parents leaving so many of their personal documents behind, or without input and help from my sister, Helen Rockman, and my cousin, Brigitte Fuchs-Bode, as well as Evy von Seemann, Georg Gaugusch, Christopher Wentworth-Stanley, Giles MacDonogh, Gerhard Heilig, Meryl Gardner, Werner Ruthofer, Pyasa David Hone, Ingrid Kurnig, Richard Donnenberg, Margaret Main, Renate Meringer, Michael and Wolfgang Wuerdinger, Andrew K. H. Smith, Mervyn Waldman, (Rocky) J.R. Bartos and, last but not least, my darling wife Ellie.

Contents

Illustrations

in traditional Austrian dress called a "Dirndl", St. Gilgen, Austria, 1951.

(17)   5 West Park Marbury, Northwich, Cheshire, UK. The bungalow as my mother would call it (actually a converted P.o.W. hut, in which we lived in from 1955 to 1963).

(18)   My mother in front of Bedford van, which my father bought because the nursery business was becoming successful. Torbay, Devon, England, summer 1958.

(19)   Gathered around Bianca Blaschke's grave, Peter, Helen, Henry and Christine Frank; Hildegard, Brigitte, Jupp, and Waldtraut Hagel and Adolf Blaschke, Warburton Old Church Cemetery, Cheshire, England, summer 1959.

(20)   The bed-sitting room business. Hartford, Northwich, Cheshire, England, 1960s.

(21)   Henry Frank with Skipper the Labrador in back garden, Hartford, Northwich, Cheshire, England, late 1960s.

(22)   Henry and Christine Frank, Northwich Sailing Club, Winsford Flashes, Winsford, Cheshire, England, 1970.

(23)   Henry and Christine Frank on their 40th wedding anniversary with their grandchildren Vanessa and Matthew, July 1980.

Introduction

When I was young my mother always told me that I had blue blood in my veins. Now, I knew from a boy across the road that if one's blood turned blue it was either through lack of oxygen or one had been poisoned, so I always thought I was about to die. It was only later that someone explained it meant I came from nobility.

My mother also told me that God had brought me into the world. I supposed this stopped me from believing what other children believed at the time, that I had been found under a gooseberry bush. When we got our first car in 1950, a 1936 Austin 16 saloon, my older sister Helen and I would argue about who of us should sit in the front seat next to the driver. I was so desperate to sit in the front passenger seat that one day I asked my mother whether, when God brought me into the world, I was sitting in the front seat. I imagined this rather mythical grey-bearded man in vicar's clothing driving a car just like ours and pointing to the planet Earth, where I was to be united with my parents and my elder sister. My mother burst out laughing and said she must write it down and send it to the Reader's Digest, of which she was an avid reader, but she did not enlighten me as to how procreation really happened. So a few days later, while my sister was playing with a couple of girls from over the road, I told them what I had asked my mother and they laughed too, and one of them said, "Don't talk daft — you grow in your mum's tummy and then you come out of her bum." Talk about being let down with a bump: one of my many disappointments in life.

My mother was born on 29th April 1918 in a village called Makoschau in Upper Silesia, in what was then known as the German Empire. After the Versailles Settlement in 1921, the western Polish border was moved westwards to include parts of Upper Silesia. Although still living in the same village, she and her family had to take Polish nationality, and the village was given the Polish name of Makoszowy.

Her family were Catholic, as was she at the time. She was born Krystyna Bianca Blaschke, but after marrying my father in England in 1940 she changed her name to Christine Bianca Frank. She also adopted the Church of England as her religion and became a naturalised British citizen in 1947.

My father, Heinrich Edmund Edgar Oscar Frank or, to give him his full title, Heinrich Edmund Edgar Oskar Ritter von Frank Labor, was born on 21st April 1914 in Vienna, Austria, to a couple who were Jewish by race but not by religion — as they had previously converted to Christianity. When my father came to England, he too adopted the Church of England religion, changed his first name to Henry and also became a naturalised British citizen in 1947. Because the changing of their first names does not appear to have happened on a precise date, I tend to use their original first names, Krystyna and Heinrich, in the earlier parts of the story and their Anglicised names, Christine and Henry, later. To describe my origins and part of my identity I always explain in a shorthand way that I am the product of a German, Polish, Catholic mother and an Austrian, Jewish, Protestant father, and that I was born in North Wales.

This story is about two families, namely Blaschke and Frank — the former from Upper-Silesia (now part of south western Poland) and the latter from what is now the Czech Republic (but having moved to Vienna sometime in the nineteenth century). It is also about how my parents came to be in England a few months before the start of the Second World War, how they met and married, what happened to them, and my experience of growing up with them both as foreigners from different European countries. By a twist of fate, I now live in Austria, the birthplace of my father.

Although this book is supposed to be about my parents, someone once told me that if you want get people's attention when telling a story, you need to give something of yourself. I therefore have to admit it is also about me and to a lesser extent about my sister Helen. Without over-emphasising, I have tried to highlight what it was like to grow up with parents from Central and Eastern Europe who had different social and cultural values from many of the people with whom we associated in rural Cheshire; parents who originated from comfortable and well-off

16

backgrounds found themselves refugees with little or no money and no family on which to fall back, and who strove to make a success of their lives in a foreign country.

My mother always wanted to tell me about her life before the war in Poland but, because of that, I did not want to know. On the other hand, my father, brought up in Vienna and born to non-practising upper-class Jews who perished in the Holocaust, hardly ever talked about his family or background and especially not about the details of how he managed to flee from Austria in May 1939. Much of what I have since learnt has been gleaned since coming to live here in Austria.

My mother's characteristics can be described as stoic, slow to anger, loyal and hardworking. She was a homemaker, a wonderful, devoted and sweet mother, and an inveterate smuggler and liar. My father was the exact opposite. He was excitable, quick to anger, clever, cultured, a great conversationalist, knowledgeable, passionate about horticulture, terrified of people in uniform (particularly police and postmen), untidy, spoilt, and had no interest in owning material items. Later in life, when thinking about them, I began to realise their relationship was like the immovable object being met by the irresistible force — my mother the stoic Pole, and my father the excitable Austrian — which made for an interesting life.

I must explain that the contents of this story are based on three sources. Firstly, the many documents and photographs that my parents left to my sister and me. Secondly, information from websites that clarified, explained and supported the statements I have made. Thirdly, and by far the most common, from my own memories of conversations with my father, mother, sister and (in some cases) with other people, particularly my cousin in Hamburg, Brigitte Fuchs-Bodde (née Hagel), and last but not least Evy Seemann (or to give her full name and title, Eva-Maria Seemann von Trauenwert). Now, I accept that much of what I heard or was told was when I was young, and I appreciate that the passing of time plays tricks on one's memory, and on those of others who recounted the incidents and stories of my parents, grandparents or even (in some cases) my great-grandparents' lives. Therefore, I cannot absolutely guarantee that what I have written is a completely true record. However, as my father wrote at the beginning of his second attempt at writing his family history, "Si none Vero est bon trovato…". I must thank Michael Würdinger, my wife's eldest nephew, who explained that my father's Latin roughly translates into English as "If it is not true [then] it is a good story."

Peter Frank. Pernitz, Austria

Chapter 1

Family Origins: German Empire and Poland

My maternal grandfather's name was Adolf Blaschke. He was of Germanic stock from the very eastern edges of what was once the German Empire, a region called Upper Silesia. His family home was in a place called (when it was part of the German Empire) Schönau in the district of Leobschütz, now known by its Polish name Grabczyce. I have a hand-written document in my archives, which he drew up in March 1951, showing the property he owned; it had been in his family for generations. It was a small farm of about 1.75 hectares consisting of three fields, a farmhouse, out-buildings and an orchard, that were rented to a tenant farmer. Adolf did not live there because he was a head forester or "Oberförster". His role included all parts of forest management, including the management of game, arranging hunting parties, felling trees, managing sawmills, the sale of wood, and so forth, for a large estate called "Neudeck bei Tarnowitz" that was not far from the town of Beuthen (now known by its Polish name Bytom).

The Neudeck estate was owned by the Henckel von Donnersmarck family, and Adolf Blaschke worked directly for the "Fürst" (or Prince in English). As head forester a house went with the job, known in German as *Das Forsthaus* or "Die Försterei". The first house he occupied with his family was an old farmhouse "with big rooms and a huge kitchen, which had beams across the ceiling", according to my aunt's memoirs, in Makoschau in Upper Silesia. Adolf Blaschke was born on 30th October 1877, presumably at the family home in Schönau, and died in the village of Allesberg, south of Nuremburg, in Bavaria on 26th August 1960. I have no real information about his early life except for a few of his experiences during hunting events before World War I, when he as a young man and he assisted the head huntsman (gamekeeper) of the then Fürst von Donnersmark.

I remember my maternal grandfather as a tall man with a bald head and a very impressive large white beard. In his later life he was once mistaken for George Bernard Shaw whilst staying with my mother's sister, Waldraut, in the Hamburg suburb of Blankenese, and when he visited us in England in 1954 and went out for his daily walk children would proclaim that Father Christmas was walking around without his sledge, reindeer or red cloak. I remember him wearing the traditional green/grey hunting jacket, knee breeches and knee length socks of the hunters of Bavaria and Austria, a very strange sight in the austere early 1950s in a poor area of northwest England! He was a Catholic, very strict and reserved, but he could also be kind.

My maternal grandmother's name was Bianca Blaschke (née von Radziewski). She was also born in Upper Silesia, on 23rd February 1879, and died in Warburton, Cheshire, England on 28th February 1950 (more of why and how she died there later). Her father was Hermann Oskar August Karl von Radziewski, born on 19th November 1846 in "Klein Lassowitz" and died on 1st August 1905; he was also a forester, with the job title "Königlicher Revierförtster" (King's Forester) of a particular region. He would have been a forester of very high standing — higher than that of an *Oberförster*.

Now I must stray from the subject for a moment. My mother always said to me, "Never forget you are a Radziewski", but never explained what she meant by it, except to say the family was very important and noble. In the early 1990s my cousins in Hamburg (children of my mother's elder sister Waldtraut, known to me as "Tante Trautel") gave me a copy of the Radziewski coat of arms. I never thought much more about it but the name did stick with me. Then one day, probably in 2003 or 2004, a visitor asked me about the picture of the coat of arms hanging on the wall. I explained that it belonged to the Radziewski family and that my mother's mother, Bianca, had been born Radziewski. The person expressed surprise, asking if I knew that during Oliver Cromwell's time in power he had thought about his succession and about how his successor could be chosen. The person went on to say that Cromwell heard that the Polish chose their future kings by the nobles voting one of them to succeed to the Polish throne. The person went on to say that Cromwell was in contact with the Vice Chancellor of Poland, a Cardinal

Radziejewski (note that the spelling of the name can vary depending on whether it is written in Polish, German, French or English). I traced the Radziejewski family from the time of Cromwell, and interestingly, at some time during the eighteenth century, they were exiled to Upper Silesia; unfortunately, they appeared to have died out fifty years before Hermann Oskar August Karl von Radziewski's father (Karl Radziewski) was born in 1807.

Bianca and Adolf had two daughters. The first was Waldtraut, born on 9th August 1912 in Makoschau, Upper Silesia. She married Josef Hagel, always known as Jupp Hagel (a German) in Kalety, Upper Silesia on 25th July 1935, and died on 1st December 2007 in Hamburg, Germany. The second daughter was my mother Krystyna, born on 29th April 1918 in Makoschau, who married Heinrich Frank on 24th July 1940 in Thurlestone, Devon, England. She died on Tuesday 17th June 1986 in Hartford, Northwich, Cheshire, England.

According to my aunt's memoirs, Makoschau had a kindergarten, a junior school, a post office, shops for food, and a cloth and flour mill. Following junior school, at the age of eleven, Waldtraut was sent to a German-speaking boarding school (actually a convent called the "Ursulinnen Pensionat") at Schweidnitz in Silesia. Unfortunately, once Poland had fully absorbed its Upper Silesian territory in 1922, everyone of German origin in that area had to take Polish nationality. However, Schweidnitz remained in German territory, so Waldtraut could no longer continue her education at the Ursulinnen Pensionat, because this would have meant having to buy a German visa costing 400 German marks. She was therefore sent to a convent in Beuthen. This school was also a convent, called "Die armen Schulschwestern Beuthen." She did not board at this school, instead commuting each day.

In 1923, when Waldtraut was eleven, the Blaschkes moved from the old farmhouse in Makoschau to Kalety (formerly having the German name Stahlhammer). Krystyna went to the local Polish-speaking junior school and then to a German-speaking grammar school ("Gymnasium" in German) in nearby Tarnowitz, where Polish was also taught, and she too commuted there daily. In 1935, the Blaschkes moved again, to Swierklaniec (pronounced "Schvierklannyetz" in Polish, and "Neudeck" in German) in Powiat (Polish for County) in Tarnowski Gory, Poland.

The reason why the Blaschkes moved house so often was because the Fürst von Donnersmarck saw that Adolf Blaschke had considerable ability to manage the forests and saw mills, and with the last move the Fürst wanted Adolf to be closer to him at the Hall at Neudeck (where the Fürst lived), which was the nerve-centre of the estate's forestry operations.

I can only remember a few of the things my mother told me about her life in Poland. She was six years younger than Waldtraut and, unlike Waldtraut, was initially kept at home and went to school locally by train. When she started school, at six years, old she got on the wrong train and was only saved by a kindly stationmaster, who put her on the correct one home. Also, her mother would play with her in the garden by making a telephone out of tin cans attached to string; and how, in summer, ice was brought from the ice cellar (where it had been kept stored since the winter) to be crushed and mixed with nuts and fruit to make a dessert. During that time, seasonal fruits were collected, and those that were not eaten were bottled for the winter. Those fruits that were damaged but clean would be put into a large stone jar known as a "Rum Topf", layer-by-layer according to the season, each layer being covered in sugar and topped off with alcohol. Once the jar was full, the top was put on and left for about a year. It was then strained into a bottle and the resulting liquor was delicious, but lethal.

My mother told me how she was taught the skill of smuggling by her mother because their house, although officially in Poland, was actually in the area known as "no-man's land", between the two official borders of Germany and Poland. So, when they drove with the horse and carriage to the local shops, presumably in Makoschau, they had to officially go through the border as though they were entering Poland. There they would buy not only food but also material to be made into clothes by their local dressmaker and tailor near their home. If caught, the border guards or customs officers would have charged them the duty on the cloth, and fined them. So, after having bought the cloth, they would go into the rear of the shop, remove their outer clothing and have the cloth wound round their bodies, covering it with their outer garments. Similarly, they would go into Germany and buy gramophone records, which were cheaper to buy than in Poland. Having bought the records, they would slide them into the space between the pull-up window on the door of the carriage and smuggle them back into Poland without paying duty. I will elaborate later on my mother's smuggling escapades.

Her father kept dogs for hunting, which were allowed in the house but never near the table when the family was eating. He loved the smell of cigars but did not smoke, so he would often light one and leave it to burn in an ashtray so that he could enjoy the aroma. Her father would, on Sunday afternoons, take my mother, her sister and his wife out into the woods in an open horse-drawn carriage. In early autumn they would hear the deer calling during the rutting season. Sometimes they saw male deer who had fought each other and whose antlers had become so entangled that they could not free themselves from each other. In winter, on a horse-drawn sledge (when there was much snow) they would be wrapped up in furs; often it was so cold that if one spat, the spittle would freeze before hitting the ground and making a cracking sound. Also, in winter, my mother would go skiing to the Tatra Mountains. My aunt Waldtraut told me in 1998 of a time in the late 1920s when the temperature in winter remained below minus forty degrees centigrade for over a month and the trunks of cherry trees split open.

Once, while watching television with my mother during the time of the Soviet Union, Kaliningrad was mentioned. It is now Russian sovereign territory but separated from Russia by Lithuania and Poland. My mother said that Kaliningrad used to be part of what was called East Prussia (or "Ostpreussen" in German), and was then known as Königsberg. After the Versailles Settlement it became part of the new Republic of Germany but was separated from the rest of the country by Poland. An agreement between Germany and Poland allowed Germans wanting to travel from the main part of Germany to East Prussia to do so via a special "rail corridor". Similarly, there was a rail corridor from Poland through Königsberg to the Baltic States. For some reason my mother had to travel on this rail corridor, and when the train reached the East Prussian western or southern border it would be stopped and German frontier guards and customs officers would thoroughly inspect every passenger's passport and baggage. Once this was done all the window blinds were closed and sealed. All the carriage doors were locked, and only then was the train allowed to cross East Prussia into Lithuania.

Krystyna held a Polish identity card from 20th June 1938 and a driving licence from 7th October 1938. She appears at some stage, probably while still in Poland, to have had a friend called Bernhard, because in amongst her documents was a scrap of paper (which may have been part of a longer letter), written in "Kurrent" script, from Bernhard (who wrote to her from Bucovina, then part of Rumania). Evy Seemann translated it into English, and it reads "I am ending for today — there is always someone who interrupts me — my dear Christel, best regards from your Bernhard". The sender's address is given as *poste restante* ... (Bucovina).

Later, while still in Poland, she had a friend called Joachim, of whom she was very fond and he of her. It was a serious friendship and in 1938 Joachim asked my mother to marry him. However, her father Adolf was against the marriage for some reason, and also by this time my mother had decided she wanted to work for the Polish Foreign Service. After passing her A Levels (known as "Abitur") in the German-speaking grammar school in Tarnowitz, she went for an interview with the Polish Foreign Ministry for a job as an interpreter. They told her she would be considered if she could speak a third language, preferably English or French. She already spoke German and Polish fluently.

Her father, being head forester, was close to the Fürst von Donnersmarck, the owner of the estate, who had sent his sons to Oxford University. The Fürst also had contacts at Exeter University so was able to help my grandfather secure a place for my mother, but at that time, in 1938, her English was not good enough for a University course. It was therefore decided to send her to Devon to live with a family in Bovey Tracey, starting in late January 1939, to improve her English until the course began in the October. However, she became very unhappy with her father's refusal to even let Joachim and her become engaged. Her father, seeing her unhappiness, said that if she went to England as planned and then, on her return, she still felt the same about Joachim (and he still felt the same about her), he (Adolf) would consent to the engagement and ultimate marriage. Later, it will become clear that the engagement and marriage never happened because Krystyna never did return to Poland.

Because of the war, Krystyna and Joachim were forced to go their separate ways. When my grandfather Blaschke died in August 1960 my mother flew to Allesberg for the funeral, and a local newspaper reported the event and gave my mother's name and address correctly at that time as Christine Bianca Frank, 5 West Park, Marbury, Northwich, Cheshire, England. Somehow, Joachim saw the funeral article and kept it, or at least my mother's name and address. Roll forward another five years to 1965 and Joachim, living somewhere in Germany by then, had to come to Manchester for a conference or business meeting. He happened to stay over the weekend in Manchester and, finding himself at a loose end, asked if it was possible to travel to Northwich from Manchester, which it was.

He travelled by train and when he arrived at Northwich Station, he asked for directions to Marbury; he was told that he would have to take a bus to the then bus terminus in Northwich, and from there another bus to Marbury. Now by this time my parents had moved from Marbury to Beech Road in Hartford, a suburb to the west of Northwich. On arrival at the bus station, he got on the wrong bus, which was travelling in the direction of Hartford. However, when the bus conductor asked him for his fare, and Joachim said he wanted to go to Marbury, the bus conductor explained that he was on the wrong bus and put him off at a bus stop where a different bus would take him to Marbury. Fortunately, at the bus stop he got into conversation with someone who knew my parents and explained that they no longer lived in Marbury but now lived in Hartford, and this person gave him their new address.

Whether he walked (as it was not that far) or he took another bus is not known. It was a Sunday afternoon and my parents had visitors who were old friends from when they first moved to Cheshire. My father was out with the husband, and the wife was at home with my mother. Suddenly the front doorbell rang and my mother went to see who it was. As she opened the door, she immediately saw it was Joachim, whom she had not seen since before the war. They spent some time reminiscing, while my mother's visitor found the whole situation extremely funny and could not stop giggling at the fact that my mother's teenage sweetheart had turned up on the doorstep — far away from Poland and twenty-seven years later. I don't think my mother kept in touch with Joachim after his visit. She told my sister that he had lost all his hair, and that she was so glad she had married my father (who kept his till his death in 1983).

One final thing of note: my mother was always interested in the occult, but only in so far as what the future would hold for her. She particularly liked to consult fortune-tellers or mediums to learn what would happen to her and her family. She told me that while still in Poland she visited such a person, who told her she would leave her home and travel to a far-off land where she would settle and end her days. As I have already said, she died in Hartford, Northwich, Cheshire, England. She also told me that in her later teenage years she and her friends decided to try and use a Ouija Board. They turned off most of the lights in the room and sat at a round table with letters of the alphabet arranged in order around it. They took a glass or a plate and marked it with the soot from a candle, set it in the middle of the table, and each put one finger on the glass or plate. My mother, who could be absolutely bold and fearless, asked the first question: "What is the name of my future husband?" Now, at this time she appears to have been friends with two men, Bernhard and Joachim, so I suppose she thought the answer, if any came, would be one of these two, but as the plate or glass moved it spelled out HEINRICH!

Although my grandfather's first name was Adolf during the Second World War, he was opposed to Hitler and his desire to wage war. In Adolf's "Niederschrift", an account of how he and Bianca fled Poland in January 1945 to escape the advancing Russian army, he mentions that once Hitler had attacked Russia, in the summer of 1941, he knew Germany would lose the war. He continued to openly criticise Hitler until his brother in-law, Otto von Radziewski, told him that if he did not stop, he would end up in a concentration camp.

In all other aspects the war hardly affected my maternal grandparents; life went on as normal. Their older daughter, Waldtraut, visited regularly with her then two children, Karl-Heinz and Brigitte, and with her husband too (when he was allowed leave from his job in charge of a part of the logistics and supply department of the German Luftwaffe). Adolf and Bianca's only concern was for their younger daughter, Krystyna, who had been sent to England in January 1939 to improve her English before enrolling on an English course at Exeter University.

Krystina's Polish passport shows that she left Poland from Beuthen on 21st January 1939, arrived in Belgium on 24th January, boarded a cross-channel steamer at Ostend and landed in Dover on 25th January 1939. She had in her Polish passport transit visas for Germany and Belgium, and a British student visa valid for one year. On the last page it shows that she had what appears to be 20.70 Belgian francs, seven English pounds, and one unit of another currency (possibly Zloty) bought or ordered from Deutsche Bank in Katowice on 20th January 1939. It appears her father had paid for this currency with two hundred German Reichmarks.

In Dover she would have taken the train, probably to Victoria, then crossed to Paddington Station where she would have taken the train to Newton Abbott. In March 1939, when Germany invaded Czechoslovakia, people in the UK began to talk about the possibility of war, so my mother wrote to her father saying that she wanted to return home. Being the stern authoritarian that he was, he replied that she was just homesick and that nobody was talking about war where he lived, so she should stay put. As things worsened in the early summer, my mother wrote again asking if he would send money so she could return home. My grandfather only sent enough money to my mother every month to pay for her keep with the family she lived with, and some pocket money.

Then, in the third week of August, the German army was mobilised and my grandfather finally realised things were very serious, so he sent my mother a telegram to the effect that she should return home immediately — travel money and tickets were on the way. Unfortunately, war was declared on Sunday 3rd September and the money and tickets arrived on Monday 4th September. The borders were closed and my mother was stranded in England.

The return ticket, which was never used and which I still have, was issued by the Polish travel agency ORBIS. It had her travelling from London to Dover with the Southern Railway, Dover to Ostend by boat, then again by train from Aachen to Berlin, and finally from Berlin to Beuthen. There is no mention of how she was to get from Devon to London or from Ostend to Aachen; presumably she was to buy tickets with the money her father had sent, and she would also have had to pay for transit visas for Belgium and Germany.

Looking at the portion of the ticket from London to Dover, it can be seen that it was issued by Hungarian State Railways. I asked Werner Ruthofer, who used to work for Austrian State Railways, why this was so. He gave a possible explanation that neither the Polish Travel Agency ORBIS, the Polish State Railways, nor German State Railways had the capability to issue such a ticket, only Hungarian State Railways. A second possibility was that World War II was so imminent that only Hungarian Railways still had an agency agreement with Southern Railway.

Werner went on to explain that separate state railway companies and travel agents had the capability to contact each other via Morse Telegraph, and so it would be possible for ORBIS to contact the Hungarian State Railways and have that portion of the ticket sent from Hungary to Katowice by the next train. On receipt, ORBIS would send payment by the return train.

What happened to my mother after 3rd September 1939 is part of Chapter 4. My grandparents had no contact with her apart from three Red Cross messages sent via Geneva, the first arriving in January 1942. They knew she was in the area near Plymouth and they often heard on German state radio how badly that part of England was bombed, so they feared the worst.

How they finally managed to contact her again is also described in Chapter 4. My mother told me a story about the first Red Cross message she sent. My mother said that she did not write, "Am married have a daughter Helen. How are you? Love Christine", as grandfather Blaschke claimed in his "Niederschrift". She actually wrote, "Married Henry July 1940 daughter Helen born October 1941. How are you? Love Christine." Unfortunately, in Geneva (probably) the message was transposed stating, "Daughter Helen born October 1940 married Henry July 1941". When she met her father (a strict Catholic) several years later, although pleased to see her he was a little cool towards her. On asking her mother why this was, Bianca explained the reason. My mother, a very open-minded person, laughed and explained that she had married Henry in July 1940 and Helen had been born in October 1941. Once this had been explained to her father his attitude to my mother changed completely.

In January 1945 my maternal grandparents had recently celebrated Christmas and New Year with Waldtraut and her then two children, Karl-Heinz and Brigitte. It became clear that the Russians advancing from the east would overrun where they lived. My grandfather was determined to remain but at the last minute, when the Russian artillery could already be heard, he decided to leave. He was finally persuaded by Bianca to flee.

On 20th January 1945 they packed what they could onto a horse-drawn open shooting-brake, closed the door of the house behind them and at 4 p.m. drove off westwards into a very cold January night. The full story of this journey is told in what he called his "Niederschrift". I have to thank Gerhard Heilig for translating it into English.

I only knew Bianca for a very short time, when I was four years old, so I can't remember much about her except she was a very kind person. The reason for me having known her, and why she died in Warburton, Cheshire, is that Bianca and Adolf Blaschke came to visit us in Warburton in January 1950. Their visit is described in more detail in Chapter 5. After that I saw my grandfather again in 1951 when we visited him in Allesberg. He visited us in April and May 1954 and again in 1959, then I saw him for the last time again in Allesberg, northern Bavaria, Germany, as he was about to die from stomach cancer in the summer of 1960. I can't remember much about him. I was never able to communicate with him and so knew little about who he was.

Chapter 2

Family Origins: Austrian Empire

My paternal great grandfather was Demeter Frank, born on 29th July 1829 in a place called Horschitz (known by its Czech name Horice), east of Prague in what is now the Czech Republic. It was then in a region of the Austrian Empire called Bohemia. He died in Milan at the end of November 1909 and is buried there in the "Cimitero Monumentale".

His mother, Josefa Frank (née Pick), was born in 1804 in Patzau, Tabor in Bohemia; she died in Türkenstrasse, Vienna, Austria on 3rd October 1884 and was buried on 6th October in the Jewish section of the Vienna Central cemetery. I am grateful to Georg Gaugusch of Vienna for finding Demeter's and Josefa's graves.

Demeter's father Joseph Frank was born in Horschitz in 1801; I do not know when he died. Josefa and Joseph married on 27th August 1828 in Horschitz and had five children: Demeter, Adolf, Babette, Isidor and Ignatz. They were a Jewish family. Joseph was a wealthy man, owning property and mills in Bohemia. He ensured his children were well educated and could ride. His financial downfall came when fat left in a hot oven began to burn. The fire spread through the chimney and out into the fields. At this time there was no fire brigade and the whole estate went up in flames. The shock was so great that he died soon after.

Demeter came to Vienna to study at Vienna University at the time of the 1848 revolution in Austria. He was a member of the Academic Legion, part of the Civil Guard, which was meant to keep order and stop the rioting mob plundering the suburbs. Demeter was standing in Josefsplatz as bombs exploded and the roof of the palace library caught fire. The mob were advancing very quickly, so Demeter and his friend tore off the military insignia from their clothes and ran to a building in Bäckerstrasse, where one of his professors had a flat, and they remained hidden there for several days.

Demeter then escaped to Moravia, now part of the Czech Republic, and went to a town called Kremsier where a parliament, originally convened in Vienna, had moved because of the revolution. The parliament was writing a constitution to turn the absolute monarchy of the Austrian Empire into a constitutional one. While Demeter was at university, he had learnt to be a stenographer and had wanted, after university, to become a court stenographer. He worked for the Kremsier Parliament as a stenographer taking dictation as the constitution was discussed. Unfortunately, the constitution was very short-lived as the parliament was dissolved in March 1849 and the Austrian Empire remained an absolute monarchy.

Later Demeter went to Paris and took a job with the Banque Ottomane. He then went to Constantinople, now called Istanbul, where (in partnership with a man called Siegfried Adler) he set up first an import and export business and then a merchant bank (which was involved in the financing of the Orient Express railway line from Vienna to Constantinople).

It was either in Paris or Constantinople that Demeter met Carl von Morawitz, his future son-in-law. Thanks to Christopher Wentworth-Stanley's research, I now know that Morawitz arrived in Paris in 1868 and joined the Bank Bischoffsheim & Bamberger. He then moved to the Banque Ottomane in Paris in 1870. In 1871 Morawitz became secretary (in modern terms, the finance and administration manager) and later right-hand man to Baron Maurice de Hirsch, a Bavarian. Hirsch had been negotiating with the Ottoman government to build a railway from Vienna to Constantinople.

An alternative possibility is that Morawitz met Demeter in Constantinople. My father always said that Demeter was ennobled because he helped with the financing of the last stretch of the Orient Express railway from Vienna to Constantinople. However, my father's mother, Ilona Frank, in her "Family Memories" written in January 1937, states that Demeter was officially ennobled because "he was a long-standing chairman of the Austrian Relief Action Committee". Ilona goes on to say that the reason for him being given the Order of the Iron Crown and his title was that "he worked for Austrian diplomats [providing] reports [which served] as documents for the consuls' commercial reports". He also provided the Austrian ambassador with secret information, as he was friendly with the private secretary and several relatives of the Romanian King.

During a holiday in Alexandria in Egypt, Demeter met Leonie de Tedesco, who was born in Milan on 30th January 1847 and died in Sèvres, France in August 1879. Her family were French. He fell in love with her and asked for her hand in marriage. She accepted and they were married in Paris on 8th June 1865. The only evidence I have found of any Jewish religion in the Frank family relates to the Hebrew prayer book given to Leonie Tedesco by her mother at the time of her marriage to Demeter Frank. They were photographed together in Constantinople. They had four children, three born in Constantinople (Paul, Margarethe and Edmund) and a fourth, a girl born in December 1878 in Bucharest but who died aged two months. Edmund was my grandfather.

At some time in the 1870s, Demeter and Leonie moved to Bucharest so that he could take up the position of General Director of the Banque Roumane. They mixed with the very highest of Bucharest's society, which included high-ranking diplomats, financiers, and powerful families such as the Baltazzi, Bratianu, Dumbas and Stirbey. They also attended the court of King Carol, because he was the chairman of the Banque Roumane.

A family rumour says that Leonie was very unhappy with the move from Constantinople, where she loved the cosmopolitan lifestyle, and hated Bucharest because it was so parochial. As a result, Demeter immersed himself in his new job and the couple grew apart.

Allegedly, Leonie began an affair with one of the Princes of Liechtenstein, which resulted in her being pregnant with Edmund. In my father's very sparse papers concerning family history he states that his father Edmund was born in 1870, not in 1872 as official records show. My father's papers go on to state that Edmund had two birth certificates, which my father says he saw, one showing Edmund to have been born in 1870 and the other giving the date in 1872. He was given the Christian names Johann Edmund or Edmond, as his mother (who was French) liked to call him, on his first birth certificate but only Edmund on his second dated 1872. According to my father's papers, Johann is the first Christian name of all the male line of the Liechtenstein royal family.

Evy von Seemann and Marietta (Ditti) von Puscariu confirmed this story when I met them in St. Gilgen in August 2011. They both knew Edmund, as Evy was his great niece and Ditti was Evy's half cousin. They both told me the same story that Edmund tried to use this as a reason not to be branded as a Jew by the Nazis after the Austrian "Anschluss" in March 1938. He tried, unsuccessfully, to claim that although his mother was Jewish, his supposed real father was a Prince of Liechtenstein and as such he was of mixed race and therefore should not have been classified as a Jew. Interestingly, in 1883 Demeter bought a small castle from Prince Philipp of Liechtenstein, near St. Gilgen in Austria.

It is said that the last child, born in December 1878 in Bucharest and who died two months later in early 1879, was meant to be a sign of Demeter and Leonie's reconciliation. Sadly, Leonie died of pneumonia while on holiday in France in the summer of 1879 (apparently because her spirits were very low due to the death of the child, and she had lost the will to live).

After Leonie's death, Demeter did not socialise widely in Bucharest society. However, he did invite high-ranking men to his house for what were known as "Café" evenings, where they could talk about business and political affairs and for amusement played billiards and cards. Many who came were diplomats such as the Austrian Ambassador, Count Goluchousky, and the British Ambassador Mr White. These evenings allowed for informal discussions on foreign affairs, allowing many issues to be resolved.

Demeter remained in Bucharest into the 1890s. He received several decorations, the first of which was the Iron Crown and title "Ritter von" (Knight of) from the Austrian Kaiser, Franz Joseph. He also received Romanian decorations such as the Star of Romania and even a German Medal of the Eagle decoration. Demeter was a Freemason, possibly a master or grandmaster.

When Demeter left Bucharest, he went to live in Vienna and then to Milan, where he died in 1909. I once asked my father what happened to all Demeter's money and he said he wasn't sure, but he had been told that the eldest son Paul was due to inherit but had then decided to become an artist and left Vienna for Milan, so Demeter gifted much of his fortune to my grandfather Edmund (who promptly spent most of it in a relatively short time). Disgusted with Edmund, Demeter went to Milan, where he may have left the remainder of his fortune to Paul and his daughter Margarethe.

My grandfather, Edmund, came to Vienna in the late 1880s and studied law — gaining a doctorate. He converted to Christianity by being baptised on 27th June 1893 in Vienna. He then went for his military training to the officers' academy in Wiener-Neustadt. Afterwards he was sent by his father to Trieste to learn to be a banker, but he hated the parochial and provincial life and so returned to Vienna where he became an official in the Austrian Tobacco monopoly.

He appears to have resigned from this position at the end of October 1905, probably soon after Demeter gave him the money. Therefore, while still in his mid-thirties he lived a life of leisure. After leaving his job he began to receive a pension from 1st November 1905 at the grand old age of thirty-two and eleven months. In his "Verzeichnis über das Vermögen von Juden" (Register of a Jew's property, both fixed and moveable) that had to be completed by Jews during the Nazi era, he declares that the pension in 1938 was worth 972 Reichmarks per year.

At about forty, with most of his fortune spent, Edmund began to look around for a rich woman whom he could marry. While riding in the Prater in 1913 he met Ilona Fischl, born in Vienna on 16th January 1880. They married in Vienna on 23rd June 1913. Edmund never worked again. His main preoccupations appear to have been conversation, skiing, rowing and women. Evy von Seemann confirmed Edmund's womanising when we visited Vienna together and were walking past the Sacher Hotel, which is behind the State Opera House. She said when ballet was being performed in the Opera House, Edmund would invite female dancers to the Sacher Hotel.

Later in Ilona and Edmund's marriage, when money was short or more likely Ilona would no longer finance him, Edmund would while away his days in a Viennese coffee house. He would order a coffee, which always came with a glass of water. These he would make last several hours while he read all the newspapers freely available in the establishment. To extend his stay even longer he would order a second free glass of water, which one was allowed to do. The waiter would bring it and bang it down on the table because, as always, Edmund had overstayed his welcome. Edmund organised a bridge club and is supposed to have run a marriage agency in the same coffee house.

My father said Edmund and Ilona's marriage was one of convenience, where Ilona supported Edmund's lavish and wayward lifestyle and Ilona got access to Edmund's title and an agreement that they would have a child. On 14th March 1918 Edmund raised the family title from Ritter von Frank to Ritter von Frank Labor, with the family motto "Per Laborem ad Honorem" meaning "honour in work". His credentials are given as "Doctor of Laws, a retired executive revenue officer, former Lieutenant, landed gentleman, volunteer in the War Ministry's War Welfare Office, bearer of the 'Kriegskreuz für Zivilverdienste dritter Klasse' (i.e. War Cross) for Meritorious Civilian Service Third Class".

At some point in time, a portrait of Edmund was painted, of which to my knowledge only a picture postcard still exists. For many years it was in my parents' house. I thought it was a small photograph in a metal frame of Edmund sitting in a chair. On the death of my mother I took it to my own home and have had it ever since. It is unknown what happened to the painting.

My father Heinrich Edmund Edgar Oskar was born in Vienna on 21st April 1914 and was christened on 1st June 1914 in the Evangelical Reform Church. He died in London on 4th September 1983 in the Royal Masonic Hospital, Hammersmith, London. On his christening/birth certificate it shows his parents as belonging to the same church.

Ilona Fischl, who was to become my grandmother, was one of six children born to Gustav Fischl (a banker born in Budapest on 9th December 1835, who died in Vienna on 18th June 1897) and Mathilde Fischl (née Redlich, born in Bohemia 25th April 1835, who died in Vienna on 18th December 1905). I have Ingrid Kurnig and Richard Donnenberg to thank for finding the Fischl family grave in the Jewish section of the Vienna Central Cemetery. Mathilde's parents were wealthy sugar barons who had land in Bohemia, where they grew sugar beet and had sugar factories. There were five other Fischl children: Oskar, Leo, Rinka (Katherina), Nolda and Josefina.

I don't know much of Ilona's early life, except that she rode horses. She had an English governess called Miss Wills. In the early 1900s Ilona passed her driving test and visited England and Scotland several times. She appears to have been in London in late August 1912 because friends or relatives in Baden, Austria, sent a postcard to her address at Seilerstätte Strasse, Vienna. The postcard was redirected to her at the address of Queen Anne's Mansions, St. James' Park, London, S.W.

According to my father's very brief and curtailed memoirs, while in England Ilona rode to hounds with hunts such as the Quorn in Leicestershire. He goes on to say that she had a difficult time during his birth, such that afterwards the doctor told her that her riding days were over. So, she took up driving a four-in-hand through Vienna.

The only thing I can add to the above concerns a family bible that was in my parents' home for as long as I can remember. It was in English, so I assumed they had acquired it in England before I was born or early on in my life. After my mother died in June 1986, my sister and I were sorting out the contents of her house when we came across the bible and I decided to keep it for sentimental reasons.

In 1996, after the marriage with my first wife had ended in divorce, I moved into a flat and while unpacking came across the bible. It fell open at the first page, where there was an inscription and several references to verses in the bible; the inscription states: "To Ilona Fischl with the very best wishes of her friend Sydney Selwyn Vicar of Sherborne Dorset".

There is a list of vicars at Sherborne Abbey, engraved on a plaque of stone mounted on the left inside of the porch. Sydney Augustus Selwyn, to give him his full name, was vicar of Sherborne Abbey Church from 1908 to 1916. Whether Ilona met Selwyn in Vienna or in Sherborne, or elsewhere, is not known (nor is when they met). But what is certain is that it was sometime between 1908 and her marriage to Edmund Frank, because Selwyn refers to her as Ilona Fischl (her maiden name). Also of interest, is the red sticker on the inside of the back cover of the family bible. It states "T.B. Banks & Co., College Bookseller, Stationers, Printers, Account Book Manufacturers, Bookbinding etc. High Street Guernsey".

I visited Sherborne, in the county of Dorset, in June 1997 and took a photograph of the list of vicars, after which I went across to the vicarage and asked the then-current vicar (The Reverend Eric Woods) if he had any knowledge of Selwyn. He asked why I was interested and I showed him Selwyn's inscription and references in the bible, and explained that Ilona Frank's maiden name, Fischl, had been my grandmother's and that I was trying to discover if there was any evidence that she had actually visited Sherborne. He read the inscription and references and asked, "Is there any chance that your grandmother was Jewish?" I replied, "Yes" and asked him how he had known, and he replied, "Because the verses Selwyn references suggest that he was trying to persuade your grandmother to convert to Christianity." What is interesting about this is that Ilona converted to Christianity by being baptised on 31st May 1913 and was married to Edmund on 23rd June 1913 in a protestant church, and they had their son christened in the same church. Whether Ilona, at the time she met Selwyn, was still practicing the Jewish religion is not known.

I went on to ask if the vicar knew of any local hunts in the area. He replied that there were, but he personally did not know their names or where they were. I explained that my grandmother had been a very good horsewoman in her time before she was married, and that in my father's attempts at writing the family history he had mentioned she had ridden with the Quorn, which hunts in Leicestershire. The vicar replied that he remembered that the old vicarage, demolished sometime after the Second World War, was an enormous rambling 17th or 18th century building with extensive stables, and that it was quite possible that horses used for hunting would have been stabled there and therefore that (given the period) it is quite possible that Selwyn had hunted.

At that point the vicar could not help anymore so my wife, Ellie, and I set out to explore the town. We went into the Three Wishes Coffee shop and Restaurant in Cheap Street, where we got talking to the owners (a Mr & Mrs Pinkney). I explained that I was trying to find any information or evidence of Ilona having been in Sherborne in the very late nineteenth or early part of the twentieth centuries. They suggested that I contact a Mr. Gerald Pitman of Higher Cheap St., as he was Sherborne's local historian. I wrote to him and he replied, but unfortunately his letter did not take me any further forward.

Then I received a postcard from Mr. Pitman, which gave me the name and address of someone who was a contact for the local Blackmore Vale Hunt (a Count E. De Pelet). I wrote to the Count and he kindly replied on 13th July 1997, but unfortunately that also turned out to be a dead end.

Then in January 2006 Ellie and I attended a dinner in Vienna where we sat at a table with visitors to Austria who came from Dorset, a Mr. & Mrs. Fitzgerald, and I again retold the tale of Ilona's possible visit to Dorset, meeting Selwyn and possibly riding with the Blackmore Vale Hunt. They were interested in my story as they rode with the hunt, and suggested I write to the Dorset County Records Office, which I did. Unfortunately, I have either mislaid or don't appear to have had a reply from the Records Office. Also, Mrs. Sarah Fitzgerald said she would contact the archivist at Sherborne Castle, which she did. Unfortunately, that too drew a blank and since then I have not pursued the matter any further.

Chapter 3

Family Life, Austro-Hungarian Empire and Austria

As I have already said, within less than a year after Ilona's marriage to Edmund, they had a son called Heinrich (who later in England became Henry) but because his second name was Edmund the family all called him Teddy, after the name Edward Bear. As was fashionable at the time in Vienna, his mother engaged an English governess or nanny, also called Miss Wills, to care for him. Therefore, one of his first languages was English. Even though he was born over two months before the beginning of World War I, Miss Wills remained with him throughout the War, as did many English governesses and nannies in Vienna who also survived unhindered.

His father spoke French to him because his mother (Leonie) had spoken French to him when he was young. It is possible that Heinrich's mother, Ilona, spoke English to him — especially when in the company of Miss Wills. He may only have spoken German but actually used Viennese dialect with the servants and, when he was old enough, with friends with whom he played. Therefore, he may have only begun to learn High German (or written German, as it is known in some parts of Austria) when he started school at the age of six.

Life was very good for the Frank family for the first two or three years after Heinrich's birth. Ilona had a flat in Seilerstätte in the First District of Vienna, as did her other siblings such as Oskar and Leo. In fact, Ilona's father, Gustav, had owned the whole house and presumably it was divided into flats so that each of his children had a flat as they grew up. Ilona and Edmund began married life there and my father was born in that same apartment. But, as the First World War progressed, things became financially more difficult and my grandfather Edmund sold the small castle above St. Gilgen that he had inherited from his father, Demeter. He sold it to his sister, Margarethe, who gave it to one of her daughters Thea, who was married to Alexander (or Albin) Urban.

Also, about the same time Ilona, Edmund and Heinrich moved out of Seilerstätte to a flat in Jacquingasse in the Third District of Vienna. There was a need for money, so Ilona sold the flat she owned in Seilerstätte. The Jacquingasse flat was rented for 669 Austrian Schillings per quarter and had 13 rooms. The money from the sale of the castle and the Viennese flat was used to support their lifestyle as an upper class ennobled family in the last days of the Austro-Hungarian Empire.

As World War I came to an end, food became very expensive and in short supply in Austria, and especially in Vienna. So, Ilona and Edmund bought a farm in a place called Strass near a town called Wels in Upper Austria, where they could spend the summers living off the land and in winter have food sent to them when they were in Vienna.

About this time, the family acquired a bulldog, which was quite aggressive to other dogs. Once, when my father was a young boy of four or five, he was walking in the street with the dog on a lead. Suddenly the dog saw another male dog across the street and immediately wanted to attack it. Without more ado the bulldog began to run across the street with my father still holding the lead, which by this time he could not let go of, so the dog dragged him across the street — badly scratching him down his front.

A funnier story about the dog concerned its love for cherries. At the farm there was a cherry tree which bore a lot of fruit, and my father would encourage the dog to eat the fallen cherries, stones and all. Within an hour or two the effects were quite amazing, as the dog began to urgently evacuate its bowels because of the amount of cherries it had eaten — the stones would come out with such force that it sounded as though the dog's rear end was a machine gun. Unfortunately, the farm was not a successful venture and soon began losing money, so it was sold at a loss.

Amongst the other stories my father told me was one about his Aunt Rinka, his mother's sister, who came for a visit one day and, on seeing my father looking pale and listless, she diagnosed (with no medical qualifications) that he probably had worms, and immediately prescribed a diet of garlic soup that my father was to eat every day until cured. After several days of the diet he finally managed to persuade his mother that

40

he did not have worms, and his mother stopped giving him the soup. However, for the rest of his life he could not bear to eat or smell garlic.

In Vienna even the well-off would use public transport to travel within the city. So it was with Ilona and Edmund, who would use the trams and buses. Children could travel for free if they were under a certain height. One day my father, who was still under school age, got on a tram with his father. As the conductor came to collect the fares he said to Edmund "and the child (meaning Heinrich), is he still under the prescribed height?", to which Edmund replied, "Oh yes." Heinrich, who was very proud that he was tall for his age, immediately said, "No, I am already taller" and proceeded to give his height, which was more than the height at which children could travel for free. So, a very embarrassed Edmund had to pay his son's fare.

While still quite young, perhaps six or seven, Edmund taught my father to play chess. They would play after lunch, as it was at that time that Edmund enjoyed to smoke a particular dark, strong cigar. My father was fascinated by the cigar and wanted to try it, but quite rightly Edmund refused to let him. But my father pestered and pestered his father, so one day, after Edmund had said no for the "nth" time, he gave my father the remains of the still burning cigar and told him not to try smoking it, that he should take it to the toilet to dispose of it. Of course, once out of his father's sight, he immediately tried to smoke it. The cigar made my father very ill for the rest of the day, to the extent that (unlike many of his friends) he did not begin to smoke until his late teens or early twenties. He said he only began to smoke heavily once he came to England, because he then lived with another Austrian refugee who smoked heavily. I can only remember him smoking a pipe, which he inhaled. He would smoke a tin of Three Nuns tobacco in two or three days, and before the "Ronson Variflame" gas lighter came on the market he would use a whole box of matches (fifty two in total) lighting and relighting his pipe all day.

In the late 1960s bell-bottom trousers came into fashion, and we were discussing this with my father when he told us how they had been in fashion when he was in his late teens or early twenties. He said he was embarrassed to be seen out of doors with his father because he continued to wear the narrow trousers that had been in vogue years before.

Regarding male fashion and style, my father told me that once he became a young man-about-town in Vienna he began to visit families who were friends of his parents, especially those who had a daughter to whom he was attracted. He would always wear a suit and leather gloves on such occasions. To be precise, he explained, one wore the left glove and carried the right one in the left hand. So, when one met the people you were visiting you could shake them by the hand without the delay of having to remove one's right glove.

I don't know much about my father's early life except that the family found itself in straightened circumstances after the farm was sold; the money they received from its sale soon disappeared due to the raging inflation in Austria in the early 1920s. As an aside, and an example of the rate of inflation at that time, where I now live in Austria a small piece of land was sold in the early 1920s from one neighbour to another, and by the time the transaction was completed it is said that the money for the land would only buy a loaf of bread.

Ilona had a private income from stocks and bonds, presumably left to her by her father, and Edmund had only his pension from working for the government tobacco monopoly. But the family still had at least three servants, namely a maid for Ilona (who helped her with dressing and washing), a butler (who had similar duties for Edmund) and a cook. In trying to illustrate how big the flat in Jacquingasse was, my father once told me that the dining room was sufficiently large that in winter (when there was too much snow to go out and ride his bicycle) he was allowed to ride around the dining room table.

By this time Ilona and Edmund's relationship was not close. Evy von Seemann, the daughter of Edmund's niece Leonie, who was only two years older than Heinrich and often came to play with him. She once remembered having tea in the dining room, where Edmund sat at one end of the table and Ilona at the other, with Evy and Heinrich on either side of her. She could not remember Edmund saying anything to any of them, particularly not to Ilona.

Unlike other children of his social class, my father was sent to state schools. Evy, for instance, had private tuition in French and English — not that my father needed it in those particular subjects. He may have been quite a model student. The only example of his wrong-doing in school is a very short informal note that his mother wrote to Heinrich's school, confirming that her son Heinrich Frank of form 5a had whispered.

In September 1925, at the age of eleven, Heinrich began to attend the State Technical School No.6 in the 4th District of Vienna. He remained there for seven years until June 1932, having passed the matriculation examination in twelve subjects: Religion, German language, French, English, History, Geography, Mathematics, Delineating Geometry, Physics, Chemistry, Freehand Drawing and Gymnastics. This entitled him to study at a college for engineers so that he could become a professional engineer. Unfortunately, it was the height of the depression and there was very little work even for professional engineers.

Through his mother's Redlich family contacts in the sugar industry, he managed to secure a position in the commercial office of the Sugar-Beet Factory in Enns, Upper Austria, where he was to do statistical and payroll calculations. However, because his education had been, until then, very engineering-based it was decided that he should, before starting the job, attend a one-year course of commercial studies — which he did at the Commercial Academy of the Viennese Commercial Community (Society). This he did from September 1932 to June 1933. My father once said that the employment situation was so bad when he was leaving the Academy that in his class of thirty, only he and two other students had jobs.

He started with the sugar factory on 1st September 1933 and remained there in the same position until 30th June 1938. Actually, two days after the Nazis entered Austria in March 1938, he was forbidden to enter the factory again because, although christened, he and his parents were classed as Jews and he was not allowed to work. Fortunately, because of the family connections, they paid him for his full three months' notice period.

Margret Main, a friend of my parents, told me one further thing regarding Henry's life in Vienna. She lived in my parents' house in Hartford, Northwich, Cheshire, in England. One evening in the 1960s, when the Vienna Opera Ball was being televised live by the BBC, my father and mother invited Margret into our lounge to watch the event.

The ball begins with 60 young men and women walking on to the dance floor hand-in-hand, the women dressed in white ball gowns and the men in black-tie dinner suits. They stand in a line, one behind another, the music strikes up and they begin the first waltz of the evening. Margret watched this totally entranced. She had never seen such a spectacle before in her life and, as they began to dance, she said, "I wish I could be one of those who led out the dancers. To which my father said, "I once did."

From what my father told me his main holiday until he left school was always taken with his mother in St. Gilgen, where they would go for most of the summer holidays and where my father first learned to sail on the Wolfgangsee. Evy's family had a villa by the lake but Ilona, her maid and my father stayed in the Post Hotel in the town. His sailing boat was called Swift, and he sailed every summer — especially during the regatta week. His main friends when in St. Gilgen were two of his relations, Cary (Evy's older brother) and Peter Seemann. They were second cousins to my father, and Cary and Peter were first cousins.

The last time Heinrich participated in the regatta was the summer of 1937, when Evy von Seemann was his crew. By 1937, Nazism was rife in Austria and so there was significant anti-Semitism, particularly among the sailing fraternity in St. Gilgen. Heinrich and Evy won the regatta and were presented with a cup while the on-looking crowd mainly stood in stony silence, showing their displeasure because two people with Jewish blood had won. Evy von Seemann corroborated this story when she appeared in an ORF programme (Austrian equivalent of the BBC) about Jews in St Gilgen before the Second World War. She does not mention my father by name, but she later told me she was referring to my father, and I have a copy of the programme on videotape. By the summer of 1938 the anti-Jewish laws had been fully enacted and so it was impossible for Heinrich to sail in St. Gilgen on the Wolfgangsee that year.

During the summer of 1932, as he had finished school, he went on a one or two week sailing holiday to the Baltic Sea; it was the first time he had ever seen the sea, and it appeared immense to him. He sailed on a two-masted schooner called the Albatross, which carried 260 square metres of sail. They put into Copenhagen, where he took photographs.

In the winter he skied and climbed and walked in the mountains of Austria. I remember three stories he told me about when he was skiing. In the first, he was skiing alone and was not sure of the route to take, so he went to a farm to ask. In the yard there was a very young child on top of the snow-covered manure heap. He was standing in little boots that had been nailed to two pieces of wood from a barrel. The child skied down the snow-covered manure heap right to the farmhouse door and, in the process, he did a perfect "Christie". On reaching the door, he removed the boots and hence the so-called skis, and crawled into the house. Obviously, the child could ski before he could walk!

The second story involved my father again skiing alone and being caught out in a snowstorm. Fortunately there was an empty ski hut nearby where he sought refuge, but unfortunately there was no means of heating in the hut and, as the temperature dropped, he became very sleepy; he would have probably have died of hypothermia if another very experienced skier had not stopped to check that there was no one in the hut. This person woke my father and helped him get to safety.

The last story was told to me when I was asking him about avalanches. He said that he and his friends would sometimes climb (wearing skis) steep slopes full of snow, but they would do it very quietly. The main agreement was that none of them had to talk whilst ascending or descending, as this could create an avalanche.

In early January 1933, when he was still eighteen, he took part in a climbing, skiing or walking holiday with the Austria-Youth Group of the Alpine Club. Ilona sent him a postcard. Interestingly, she appears to address her son Heinrich as Heinz. Maybe she had more than one glass of Punch at New Year? The postcard refers to a George Strakosch, who was a nephew of Sir Henry Strakosch, a friend of Sir Winston Churchill. My father and George Strakosch had obviously been friends before the war. My father often talked about George and they exchanged Christmas cards. Although George and his family lived in or near London, I met him and his wife only once — when they came to Cheshire (in the north west of England), where we lived. He came to play polo or to ride-to-hounds.

Heinrich was a very good swimmer and in summer regularly went by bus about twenty miles up the Danube from Vienna. Once there he would change into his swimming trunks and put his clothes into a waterproof bag, which he would tie to himself and then swim with the current back to Vienna.

On the 25th April 1935 he passed his driving test (for a motorcycle and motor vehicle less than 3.5 tons.); it was just a few days after his twenty-first birthday. He also took a bus holiday to what was then Yugoslavia. I have photos and postcards of the places he visited, such as Dubrovnik (then often known by its old name Raggusa) in what is now Croatia, and Budva in what is now Montenegro. He told me that the bus was a Mercedes and there was a driver and a conductor. Most of the roads in Yugoslavia were not asphalted — only the better ones had a loose gravel surface. When descending some of the steep winding mountain passes, the conductor had to operate the handbrake by throwing all his weight on to it to help with the braking as the bus entered hairpin bends, because the main brakes were not adequate for the steep road conditions.

While working at the sugar factory in Enns he would visit his parents in Vienna from time to time. Their home was quite near the British Embassy. In December 1936 the King of the United Kingdom, Edward VIII, abdicated because he wanted to marry the American divorcee Wallace Simpson. After his abdication he came to Austria so as not to jeopardize the divorce proceedings of Wallace's second divorce, which at that time was not absolute. He stayed with Baron Eugene and Baroness Kitty Rothschild at their castle in Enzesfeld, about an hour south west of Vienna. Edward regularly visited the Britsh Embassy and my father saw him in the street on several occasions.

After being dismissed from his job in Enns, Heinrich returned to Vienna to live with his parents, where he saw and heard Hitler speak from the balcony of the Hofburg Palace on 15th of March 1938. A few days later, while staying with his parents, there was a knock at the door of their flat and in walked the Gestapo, who immediately said that, as Jews, all three of them should report to the Gestapo offices the next day to be registered and to collect the yellow star that was to be sewn on to the sleeve of their coats (showing that they were Jews).

My grandmother, Ilona, and grandfather, Edmund, complied but my father, Heinrich, packed a few things and went into hiding — moving from house to house with friends, who would let him stay as long as it was safe. Although my father had no registration papers (which by law one had to carry all the time) it was safe for him to move about during the day, so he would return to his parents' flat in the daytime and make sure he returned to wherever he was staying before darkness fell.

Once, soon after he had left his parents, he returned home and his father told him that he, Edmund, was going to contest the Nazi's decision that he was a Jew (by stating that he was the illegitimate son of one of the princes of Lichtenstein, and therefore that he was of mixed race). People of mixed race were treated more leniently. Edmund went to the appropriate authority to complain and was promptly imprisoned for about three weeks before being released. While in prison he met an old friend of his who was also branded a Jew. This man had been attacked by the authorities with an iron bar, and had had one of his eyes poked out. Why this had happened my father never told me.

My sister, Helen, told me a different but more plausible story: a short time after Ilona and Edmund had registered as Jews (but my father had not), the Gestapo returned to their flat asking about the whereabouts of their son. Helen went on to tell that Heinrich was at home but had hidden in a cupboard. After some heated discussions and threats from the Gestapo, Edmund said that rather than search for his son they could take him, and that was the reason he had a short spell in prison.

It quickly became clear to my father that he had to try and get out of Austria, which after March 1938 was actually a state of Germany. The first place he tried (through his mother's relation Sir Henry Strakosh) was South Africa, where he (Strakosh) had business interests. He was offered a job as statistician within the South African Pulp and Paper Industries Limited, at its factory in Geduld near Johannesburg. The offer of a job was confirmed in a letter dated 11th July 1938 and he was to have started as soon as possible after the 1st of September 1938. Why he did not, or could not, take up the offer is unknown. I can only assume that either he or his parents did not have the money for the fare, or he could not get permission to leave Austria at that time as his papers were not in order (meaning at that time he was not registered as a Jew).

After his return to Vienna from Enns, Heinrich joined the Swedish Mission in Seegasse in the 9th District. During his time with them, he acted as an English correspondent in its emigration department, helping people in similar circumstances to himself to complete applications for visas to various countries that would possibly take Jews. Before he left for England, he obtained a reference from the mission. This also stated that he too wished to leave the country. Interestingly, he once told me that the day he finally got permission to emigrate to England he was also offered the possibility to similarly go to Sweden. He decided upon England because he spoke English and had some contacts there.

He told me that in order to emigrate to the UK as a penniless person one had to be sponsored by someone, or by some organisation, that was prepared to support you in the UK. I once asked him to contribute to a charity or good cause, and he said that he would not; I asked him why, and he replied, "If I had any spare money I would give it to the Quakers, because it was they who got me out of Austria." We were quite poor at the time, so I understood why he said what he said. I can only assume that the Quakers sponsored him because he and my mother met at "an aliens club" in Plymouth, England, in October 1939, which was organised by the Quakers. Also, they remained in contact with a Quaker family called Lawson from Devon for the rest of their lives.

During the summer of 1938 he may have worked in a guesthouse in Gloggnitz, near the Semmering in the state of Lower Austria. The establishment was called "Kurpension Harthof" and run by a woman named Evelyn Jonasz, who was the manager and/or owner. It appears that Ilona also knew Frau Jonasz, as she mentions her in a letter to Heinrich dated 20th August 1939. As a footnote to the above, Ellie and I took a bus tour in April 2017 and on the same bus was a lady called Renate Meringer from Gloggnitz. After having learnt that she was from Gloggnitz, I asked her if she knew or had heard of the Kurpension Harthof; she had not, however she was willing to enquire with the "Gemeinde" (local council) if I sent her the full address, which I did. Her reply via her husband was that she had made enquiries of the council and the council had informed her that the villa had been sold and demolished, with the intention of building several houses on the land it had occupied.

Sometime in September 1938, Heinrich began to get his affairs in order and register as a Jew in order to facilitate his possible emigration to a safe country. It was difficult, if not very dangerous, to get registered as a Jew after having been on the run from the Gestapo. He told me that he heard of a corrupt lawyer who had contacts with the Nazi authorities and who, for a fee (which included a bribe to the authorities), could resolve any irregularities regarding not having registered as a Jew immediately after the "Anschluss".

I can only assume that he used the lawyer to regularise his situation. Obviously, this required money — which he did not have. However, on discussing this with his mother, she told him she had not declared all her valuables (jewellery) when completing her "Verzeichnis über das Vermögen von Juden" (Register of a Jew's property, both fixed and moveable). He also heard of a man who would sell this jewellery on the black market, obviously taking a percentage for himself. My father took some of the jewellery to this man, who promptly sold it; this provided enough money for my father to pay the lawyer to regularise him as a Jew, and left enough over for him (when the opportunity arose) to pay for a ticket to leave Austria.

My father said that after he sold some of his mother's undeclared jewellery she asked if he could sell some more, so that she too could emigrate from Austria. So, my father took more of the jewellery to the same man and he said that he would sell it on the same basis as before, and that my father should come back in two days' time and the money would be available. The building in which the man lived was typical of Vienna at the time — it looked like a large terraced house, probably three or four stories high with a central common staircase leading to each floor, and an open stairwell. The house was actually divided into several flats on each floor.

Two days later, my father returned to the man who lived on the top floor and knocked on the door. When the man came to the door, he asked who my father was. Obviously, my father explained that he had visited the man only two days before with jewellery and now, as previously agreed, he had returned to collect the money. The man replied that he had never seen my father before and did not know what he was talking about. My father began to remonstrate with him, until he heard a commotion at the bottom of the stairs and saw several Gestapo personnel beginning to run up the stairs.

My father quickly realised that he was in great danger so turned on his heels and began to descend the stairs without drawing too much attention to himself. About halfway down he met the Gestapo, who asked if he knew whether a man lived there who was consorting with Jews by selling their valuables. My father confirmed that there was such a man who lived on the top floor in a particular flat. The Gestapo asked him how he knew this to be true and, without thinking, said that this man had just cheated him out of some money; with that, he gave a "Heil Hitler" salute to the Gestapo and continued down the stairs. Luckily at that moment the Gestapo did not think to ask him why he had dealings with the man.

The Gestapo were so keen to apprehend the man that they continued to run up the stairs. On reaching the street, my father realised he was in even greater danger because the man was bound to betray him as a Jew selling jewellery illegally. At that moment a bus passed him, going at normal speed. In those days, Viennese buses were single-decker and were open at the back. My father ran after the bus and managed to jump on; he then cautiously looked around to the house he had exited, to see some of the Gestapo coming out of the house and looking up and down the street for him. Fortunately, he managed to escape and was never caught.

One last story concerning my father's escape was one that Evy Seemann told me as we drove into Vienna one day. I happened to ask her about the hills set back from the left side of the Autobahn as you approach Vienna from the southwest. She told me they were the Vienna Woods and that it was there that she had seen my father for the last time before the war. She said the winter of 1939 had been long and cold and that in early May there was still some snow on which one could ski in the Vienna Woods, and she had gone skiing there with my father. They spent a few hours together and in all that time, although they were related and had been friends since childhood, he never once mentioned that he was hopefully about to leave Austria. She only learnt the news of his departure when she went to visit him at his parents flat, only to be told that he had gone.

I expressed my surprise that my father had not at least told Evy. She replied that that was how it was done in those days. One told as few people as possible that you were getting out in case someone betrayed you, even though your papers were supposedly in order. One did not want the authorities asking last-minute questions that might mean you missed your opportunity to escape Nazi oppression. Fortunately, Evy and my father got back in contact after the war (by letter) and she visited us in Warburton in Cheshire sometime in 1949.

My father finally received permission to leave Austria, and the papers show that he was forced to have a further middle name "Israel". He was required to detail everything he wanted to take with him, and their total value was to be less than 500 Reich Marks.

On 18th of May or soon after, he went to the West Station in Vienna "Westbahnhof", accompanied by his parents (whom he never saw again). There, Heinrich took the train to one of the channel ports (in either Belgium or France), crossed the channel and eventually arrived at London's Victoria station, outside of which was a bench where he sat, enjoying the May sunshine and thinking he was finally free and safe. His journey from Vienna to the English Channel, he once told someone, took three days; the train was often stopped by the Gestapo, who checked every traveller's papers to ensure they were in order, and was also stopped at the borders of Holland, Belgium and France by border guards.

He arrived in England on 22nd May 1939 and was sent by the Quakers to work on a farm near Devizes, in the county of Wiltshire. He stayed there only a month before asking the Quakers if they could find him somewhere more amenable. There were two main reasons for this request, the first being that he did not receive any money for his work (merely his keep) and secondly that the meal portions were very small. Several other refugees were there at the same time and there was only enough food for everyone plus one spare portion, which was given to the person who finished his food first. Up until then, like many Austrians, my father had lingered over his repast, enjoying the conversation and savouring the food. But within a few days he had learned to eat very quickly and not to engage in conversation so that he could finish before anyone else and claim the extra portion.

While there, the summer solstice occurred, probably at the very end of his stay, and he managed to borrow a bicycle and ride the seven or so miles to Stonehenge to witness the event. In those days the monument just stood in a field, with no barriers and no admission charges. Once World War II began my father was classified as an enemy alien; although classified by the Nazis as a Jew, he had come from what was now an enemy state and hence his movements were restricted and monitored.

Once my father was settled in England he managed to correspond with his parents until the outbreak of World War II on 3rd September 1939. My father actually received a postcard from his mother, sent via her friend Maria in Switzerland, in March 1940 wishing him a happy birthday.

Ilona wrote the letters in English. At the top of the letter, dated 17th July 1939, Ilona asks, "Is Mrs Fränkel still amiable or has she cooled off?" In order to explain this, I need to provide some background. Adele Fränkel was a sister of Sir Henry Strakosch. Adele Strakosch married an Otto Fränkel, who died in 1908. Their youngest child was Herbert. When Otto died, Herbert was only fourteen. Adele and Ilona were close friends and, according to Georg Gaugusch, were related by marriage. After her husband's death, Adele became short of money and Ilona, being at that time relatively wealthy, helped Adele financially and took Adele and Herbert on holiday with my father. My father once said that he found Herbert a rather uninteresting holiday companion because Herbert was several years older than he and they did not share the same interests.

When Herbert left school, he went to work for a bank in Vienna and after several years he was working in the bank's bond department. There, he and a colleague discovered that a certain bond whose market value was very low was due to mature in a few months' time, and the bond issuer was obliged to buy back the bonds at their face value plus inflation. No one but Herbert and his colleague appeared to be aware of this, so they began to buy the bonds for themselves, and when they matured, they each made a fortune.

Herbert went on to be a director of the Canadian Bank of Montreal. He appears to have got his money out of Austria before the Anschluss and by 1939 was living in a very expensive flat (in Kensington, London) with his mother, where he remained for some time. He continued to invest in stocks and shares successfully; for example, after the war he foresaw the oil boom but instead of buying shares in oil companies he bought shares in companies that made oil exploration and production equipment, and hence made another fortune.

In 1956 he bought a villa in an acre of ground in Geneva for one hundred thousand pounds. He lived there until his death in 1973. While still living in London, Herbert took on Mary Duncan as a maid and cook. When my mother and father visited Herbert and his mother in the early 1950s, Mary was present and dressed in a maid's uniform of a black dress, white apron and cap. Later, when Herbert moved to Geneva, he took Mary with him and she became his housekeeper. They then married, and Mary survived Herbert (dying in 1988 or 1989).

My father told me that on Herbert's death the villa was worth about 8 million pounds. I visited Mary in Geneva in October 1985 and in July 1987; on one of these occasions we were having lunch and somehow we began to talk about my father and how he managed to get out of Austria, and how his mother was not able to do so because the money from the second lot of jewellery was never forthcoming. Mary told me that Herbert had once told her that there was a plan to get Ilona out of Austria and to bring her to England as Mrs Adele Fränkel's companion. But Ilona required 200 pounds sterling as a deposit or bond, which was a lot of money then (current value approximately ten thousand pounds sterling). Mary went on to say that my father, on the request of his mother, approached Sir Henry Strakosch to see if he could provide the funds. Strakosch, according to Mary, refused to help. My father related this to Herbert when they met just after the war. Herbert, hearing that Sir Henry Stakosch had not helped, became very upset and said, "Why did you not come to me? — I would have gladly provided the money."

Ilona's letter, dated 20th August 1939, was the last letter from Ilona to reach my father. I am guessing that it was not sent airmail so would have taken at least five days to reach him. Even if the letter was posted on the day it was dated, it would have only arrived on the 25th or 26th at the earliest — only eight or nine days before war was declared. On 24th August 1939 the German embassy in London advised all German citizens still in the UK to leave immediately. Once war was declared, the borders closed and direct communication and travel ceased.

At some point my father did receive a copy of a letter written by Ilona to her nephew (by marriage) Edgar Morawitz and his wife Nora, dated 13th July 1940. Edgar and Nora lived in Barcelona and, Spain being a neutral country, it was possible for Ilona to correspond with them and similarly for them with Henry in England. My father and mother had a number of pieces of jewellery and other valuables that they told me mainly came from Ilona and Edmund. These items were not mentioned in Henry's final exit inventory from Austria. It is possible that they were sewn into the lining or hem of his clothing, but he would have been in great danger if he had been searched immediately before leaving Vienna. Another explanation could be that Ilona sent the jewellery to Edgar for him to forward on to my father, or that she sent it via her sister Rinka in Hungary, as she is also mentioned in the letter as having Henry's address.

What happened to Henry's parents Ilona and Edmund is altogether a different and tragic story, although at first, after Henry left, they lived comparatively well. They were perhaps short of money as they had to let out my father's bedroom, or maybe the authorities forced them to do so as Jewish property was being confiscated and commandeered. Ilona and Edmund divorced on 25th January 1940. I asked Evy Seemann and Marietta (Ditte) Puscariu if this was really the case and, if so, why. They both confirmed that Ilona and Edmund thought they would have had better chances to survive if they were divorced. Unfortunately, I did not ask why Ilona and Edmund believed that to be true. However, they both continued to live in Jacquingasse 6/4 until early March 1941, when first Edmund was moved to Liechtensteinstrasse, Vienna, and Ilona very soon after was moved to Weyrgasse, where she remained until her deportation on transport No.12 (in the direction of Minsk) in November 1941.

I have a telegram stating that Ilona Frank had been transported from Vienna on 28th November 1941 in the direction of Minsk and asking that Pastor Hedenquist of the Swedish Mission should be informed to see if he could help. I don't know who sent the telegram but it would have been someone close to both Ilona and Henry, and my feeling is that it was probably Evy Seeman. However, when I asked Evy she had no memory of it.

There are a further couple of interesting points regarding the telegram: firstly, it was originally sent to Thurlestone in Devon. The last address Ilona appeared to have had for Henry was Plympton in Devon. So, it is possible that my father communicated to his mother his change of address via Maria in Switzerland; secondly, the fact that the telegram was sent via Geneva, presumably through the Red Cross, so it took from the end of November 1941 until 12th January 1942 to arrive (having been redirected from Thurlestone to Venton House, Totnes, where fortunately someone remembered my parents had moved to Westcombe Cottage). My mother told me she remembered the telegram arriving, as she was at home with my sister, Helen, aged just over 3 months. She immediately picked up Helen and ran to where Henry was working to show him the telegram. On reading he telegram my father sat on the ground and wept.

I was told in February 1999, when visiting the Jewish Memorial "Yad Veshem" in Jerusalem, that the railway line from Vienna to Minsk ran past Auschwitz. However, when I asked Giles MacDonogh, an expert on the holocaust, he said that Auschwitz was "on the cusp" at that time. Whether Ilona survived the transport, or died during it, is not known. The last comment on the reverse side of her registration document appears to state "November 41 mit Polen..." (Removal to Poland). Above are some indecipherable letters and a date that could be 31st January 1942. On the front side of the document, bottom right, it states that her citizenship was lost (or that she lost her citizenship) in May 1944. I have since learnt that when Jews fled to a safe haven or were deported their German citizenship was revoked.

Of further interest, when examining the attachments of her "Verzeichnis über das Vermögen von Juden" one sees that correspondence about her financial affairs continues after November 1941 until April 1944, and correspondence then begins again in March 1962 until April 1962.

One of the first things that got me interested in looking into the family history was when I saw a newspaper article in the International Herald Tribune dated Thursday 22nd October 1998. In outline, it stated that the Austrian Post Office had found the equivalent of around $200,000 US in the postal savings accounts of people who had died in the Holocaust. It also stated that it had listed the people who had had accounts on a website. I asked Ellie's youngest nephew Wolfgang Würdinger, who was very good at using the Internet, if he would access the site and see if Ilona, Edmund or Henry Frank were mentioned.

He found that the name Ilona Frank was on the list so I wrote to the Austrian Post Office and, after having to send certain supporting documents of proof, they replied stating that having opened the savings box it was empty; as a gesture, they offered me twelve hundred Austrian Schillings (worth at that time approximately $100 US), which I shared with my sister. As a footnote, the Austrian Post Office conducted on each claim thorough historic research and sent me copies of the documents they found pertaining to my grandparents (some of these form the basis of this book).

After having been moved twice, Edmund was finally deported in August 1942 to the Theresienstadt concentration camp in Czechoslovakia (Terezin in the Czech language), where he died of kidney failure on 16th April 1943. It is possible that this was caused by malaria, which he contracted at an early age while living in Rumania.

I first learnt of him dying in Theresienstadt when Ellie and I visited Yad Veshem in Israel in February 1999. There I went into the Hall of Names to ask if they had any record of Ilona or Edmund. I explained that I had a telegram at home outlining Ilona's demise. This is when the woman at the enquiry desk told me that the railway line from Vienna to Minsk passed by Auschwitz. She looked on the computer but said that they had no record of either. I was just about to leave when she asked where my grandfather lived, and I replied, "Vienna." She, in a very matter of fact way (like she was giving me the time of a train), replied that he would have been sent to Theresienstadt and reached behind her for a book, which looked like an old accounting ledger. She asked again for his surname and then opened it at a certain page and said that I should look down the list on that page. There I saw Dr Edmund Frank's name and that he had died of kidney failure on 16th April 1943. It was the first time I had ever seen his name in print. I burst into tears (by nature I am not a person who cries, for example even when my parents or sister died) and my knees became weak.

Just at that moment a group of Israeli teenagers came up to the desk — they were apparently on a school trip and had a project about Yad Veshem to complete. They all had the same piece of paper in their hands and needed to obtain information from the enquiry desk as part of their assignment. They crowded around me, oblivious to my plight, with only one objective in mind, shouting in Hebrew at the woman behind the desk — she was trying to tell them to go away but they continued to be very persistent. I can't remember what happened to the young people, but I remember apologising to the woman, who replied that it was understandable. She went on to say that even then, fifty four years after the end of the Holocaust, four or five people came to her each week to report relatives who had perished. She asked me to fill in a form stating what details I had of my Jewish grandparents, which I did, explaining that they would be entered into the computer records of Yad Veshem. Then Ellie led me outside into the fresh air and sunshine.

To close this chapter, my father (after World War II) wrote on 23rd April 1946 to the police headquarters in Vienna to ask what had happened to his parents. The police headquarters must have been very short of paper at the time because they replied, by writing in ink on the reverse side of my father's typed letter, that his father had deregistered from his last address in Vienna and had gone to Theresienstadt, and that his mother similarly had deregistered and had gone to Poland.

Adolf and Bianca Blaschke with their first daughter Waldtraut circa 1916. Their second daughter Krystina (my mother) was born in 1918

Waldtraut and Krystina Blaschke mid-1920s

Coffee in the garden Krystina, Waldtraut, Bianca and Adolf Blaschke.
Kalety, Upper Silesia, Poland 06.10.1929

Leonie Frank (née Tedesco) and Demeter Frank. Constantinople (now Istanbul) 1865

Photograph of painting of Edmund Frank, name of artist and date of portrait unknown.

Edmund Frank and Ilona Fischl riding
in Vienna 1913

Heinrich Frank at 4 ¾ years old.
Note his familiar name, Teddy

Ilona Frank with family bulldog circa 1919

Edmund Frank with his son Heinrich at their farm in Strass, near Linz,
Upper Austria circa 1919

Chapter 4

England and Wales: The War Years

A few days after my mother left Poland in January 1939, she began her stay with a family at a house in Bovey Tracey in Devon. Interestingly, although having landed at Dover on 25th January 1939, according to her Alien's Registration Certificate she only reported living at Bovey Tracey on 21st April 1939. Maybe she did not know that she was supposed to report her arrival to the police at Newton Abbott until someone told her in April, or more likely she only had to report her presence within three months of arriving in England.

I know very little of her stay there, except that she was effectively a paying guest and the family may have been called Collins (as I have a photograph of a boy called Harold Collins standing in the garden of a house). On the back of the photograph is written, in my father's handwriting, "Harold Collins Bovey Tracey Summer 1939". She told me that, at first, she struggled with her English but then the wife of the family gave her an English novel to read, and after persevering for a while she said a "veil lifted" and "all of a sudden" she found English much easier.

The only other thing I remember was that somebody who was a member of a local flying club one day took her on a flight over Devon. The reason I remember this so well is because when I was young, I could never imagine that we would have the money to fly in an aeroplane — and so when she told me this story, I was very envious.

Until I studied the registration certificate in detail, I was always under the impression she resided with the same family in Bovey Tracey until after the outbreak of World War II. However, according to the registration certificate that is not the case. She left Bovey Tracey and moved to a Mrs Ching in Yelverton in June 1939, where she remained until after the beginning of World War II. Why she moved is not known.

Everything changed when war was declared because the regular monthly money from her father stopped immediately. Presumably she could not attend the English course at Exeter University because she had no means of supporting herself or paying for the tuition. However, she did have the money he had sent her for her return journey, which paid for September's and most of October's keep with Mrs Ching. But on 28th October 1939 she moved to Compton Park Road, Plymouth; I can only assume these were cheaper lodgings, and that she moved to preserve her dwindling savings, or because she realised she would have to find some form of employment — and there would be a greater chance of doing so in a city the size of Plymouth.

My mother was obviously very concerned and depressed about her plight that she would soon be penniless. But typical of my mother to cheer herself up she went out and bought herself with some of her last money a pair of silk stockings, which were very fashionable at the time before nylons became available. Modern tights or pantyhose were not even invented until much later. My father told me that when he got to know my mother around that time, she told him how she had spent some of her last money. He was furious with her for having been so frivolous. He went on to tell me that within a month or so the stockings wore out and my mother had to throw them away. Later I questioned my mother as to why she had been such a spendthrift when she was in such straightened times? Her reply was typical. She said that she knew she was about to become very poor even penniless so she thought she would have one last luxury something she had never before owned.

With her last few shillings she put an advert in the local paper stating that she was looking for an au pair or companion position, and she got a reply. She went for the interview and got the job of 'companion help' with a Mrs G.E. Cameron Wood in Whiteford Road, Mannamead, Plymouth. Before she accepted, she asked if it would be possible to eat with the family and not with the servants, to which Mrs Cameron Wood agreed.

Going back to my father, Henry Frank, I mentioned that when he arrived in England, he was sent to work for a Mr H.L. Lemon on a farm near Devizes in Wiltshire, but left there after a month. He then went to work, again as a farm labourer, for a Mr W. Ball in Elfordleigh, Plympton in Devon. He stayed, not only working but also living, with Mr. Ball for about nine months. During that time, as well as doing general farm and garden work, he was put in charge of fifty pigs. Edmund Frank, his father, refers to Henry's work with the pigs in his postcard to Henry dated 9th August 1939 — asking if Henry couldn't go barefoot while working with pigs (as was common in other countries) as it would help Henry with his sweating feet.

There are other stories relating to my father's stay with Mr Ball. The first relates to the family bible I mentioned in chapter 3. He told me that while staying with and working for Mr Ball he read the bible from cover to cover. Unfortunately, I never asked him why he did this, but I can imagine that he was very lonely and felt completely displaced from his life in Vienna; furthermore, he had no idea what might happen to him and therefore read the Bible for solace.

The second concerns my difficult teenage years. My mother criticised me for not cleaning the bathtub after having a bath. I tried to divert her criticism by saying that my father never cleaned it, so why should I? In fact, I had no idea if he cleaned it or not — I just wanted to deflect her criticism from me. She replied that my father always cleaned the bath because, when he first stayed with Mr Ball in Devon, he had not done so and in front of the family Mr Ball told my father (who had just had a bath before dinner) to go and clean it there and then. Since then my father had always cleaned the bathtub after using it. The reason he did not originally clean the bath was because in Austria there were servants that did it for him.

Sometime in late September or October 1939 the Society of Friends (better known as the Quakers) organised one evening a meeting for friendly and enemy aliens. Both my father and mother were invited separately. Once there my mother noticed a man wearing very good quality shoes. Henry and Krystyna were introduced to each other and he said, "I am the father of fifty pigs." That is how my mother and father met. My mother always said she could tell Henry was a man of breeding because of his shoes.

I have no idea how the relationship blossomed, but it did — to the point that on 24th July 1940 they married in Thurlestone Church in Devon. The witnesses were Francis Lawson, husband of Mrs J Lawson, and Maitland Tribe. On the marriage certificate my mother gives her father's name as Rudolf Blaschke, not Adolf Blaschke, and his profession as medical doctor. As one can imagine, Adolf was not a popular name in the UK at the time so she changed his first name, and because my father's father was a doctor of law she did not want to be outdone, so gave her father the profession of medical doctor rather than Head Forester, which he really was. As a result, I have often wondered if the marriage was legal and whether my sister and I were actually legitimate or not.

Other stories surrounding their wedding include my sister asking my mother if she had worn nail polish on her wedding day. She said that she had not, but instead had buffed her nails with one of the old leather nail polishers one found in manicure sets at that time. I wonder if she could have afforded nail varnish.

In a letter to my sister after our mother's death, Mrs Lawson (one of the Quakers who organised the meeting at which my parents met) states that before the wedding my father stayed with her and her husband and that her husband, Francis, gave my mother away. My father told me that on the morning of the wedding Mrs Lawson ironed the trousers of his best suit and that the Lawsons held the wedding reception at their house, and because they were Quakers there was no strong alcohol so the bride and groom were toasted with Devon cider. My parents did not have the money for a photographer so there are no proper wedding photographs.

My mother told me that Henry, although very much in love with her, was very worried that (as an enemy alien) he would be interned on the Isle of Man for the duration of the war — leaving Krystyna, if they married, to fend for herself. Please remember that although my father was classified as a Jew and had to flee to the UK, Austria after the "Anschluss" in March 1938 became a state of Germany known as the "Ostmark." Therefore, when he came to England and registered under the Aliens Order Act of 1920 he was classified as a German. His nationality was amended to Austrian on 24th December 1943.

My father's fear of being interned was resolved when he saw an advert for a job working on the Buckland Flower Farm, owned and run by a Maitland Tribe MA (Cantab), who as previously mentioned was one of the witnesses at their wedding. At the interview for the job my father explained that, although he was very keen to take the position, he was worried he would shortly be interned and so leave Mr. Tribe short-handed. At that time most able-bodied men were being called up, and labour for non-essential work such as flower growing was in very short supply. Mr Tribe replied that he had a solution to the problem, explaining that he was a special policeman and as such he would tell the authority that decided who should be interned that he would personally watch Henry and ensure he did not try to do anything criminal to endanger the UK war effort. As a result, my father started at Buckland Flower Farm around March or April 1940.

He enjoyed the work and learned a lot about the cultivation of flowering bulbs. However, there was an interesting twist regarding criminality. The Devon and Cornwall coastline has always been notorious for shipwrecks. In fact, the coastal population of both counties saw it is as a God-given right that, when a ship ran aground, they could loot the ship of its cargo and other items. While in the employ of Mr. Tribe, a ship was wrecked on a beach near the flower nursery and Mr. Tribe told my father that as he was a special policeman it was his job to go and guard the ship against potential thieves. He also asked my father to go with him to stand guard on the beach while he, Tribe, climbed on to the ship to see if anybody was stealing from it. Tribe went on the ship and after a little while came back carrying various objects. To my father's horror, Tribe then said, "OK, I have got what I want, we can go home now, and I will hide these in my house." So, effectively my father had been aiding and abetting criminal activity. My father kept in touch with Mr Tribe for several years, mainly through Christmas correspondence. The last communication I have from Tribe to my father is dated 21st December 1946.

Another story that happened while he was working for Mr. Tribe related to the control the police exercised over "enemy aliens" such as my father. One Saturday afternoon, after having worked in the morning, he went into Kingsbridge to see a film at the local cinema. He was not allowed to be out during the evening unless he obtained police permission. Therefore, he had to watch the matinee performance. He had just bought his ticket when the police, who were looking for another enemy alien who had failed to report within the prescribed time limit, stopped him from going in to see the film. They interviewed him and checked his papers thoroughly and while doing so made several telephone calls to check his credentials. By the time the police had finished with him the film had ended and all he could do was go home; he was not refunded his entrance money and, as it was the last day of the week that the film was being shown, he never did get to see it.

After the wedding, my parents could not afford to go on honeymoon, so they went directly to the property they had rented in West Buckland, Kingsbridge, Devon. My father was still working for Mr Tribe, but he was only paid two pounds a week, and at that time my mother was not in paid employment. So, sadly, Henry had to look for work which paid more, and he heard of a bulb nursery in North Devon called Sandy Lane Farm, in Braunton, that paid two pounds ten shillings a week. So, he produced a curriculum vitae as part of the job application. There is no indication as to which job he was applying for and, interestingly, he does not mention that he was doing a correspondence course for the Royal Horticultural Society's General Examination in Horticulture; he does mention that he was working "at a first rate flower farm; speciallity (sic): Narzissi (sic)". The likelihood is that he wrote the CV while still working at Buckland Flower Farm. He got the job at Sandy Lane Farm and suddenly he had increased his weekly wage by twenty-five percent! Henry and Christine moved to Braunton in August 1940.

The work at Sandy Lane Farm was very hard. For example, when the workers planted the bulbs, they were each allotted specific rows in the field to do so. A horse and cart full of boxes of bulbs came to your row and one had to take a box of bulbs off the cart as it went by, and you had to have planted all the bulbs in the box by the time the horse and cart came back to you (for you to put the empty box on the cart and take a fresh full box, without causing the driver to stop the cart). It was cold and back-breaking work. If you had not finished planting your box of bulbs before the horse and cart returned (so that it had to stop) you were heavily criticised by the foreman. If you stopped it a second time you were "sent up the road", meaning you were sent home and received no pay for that day.

There was a similar process (but in reverse) when the flowers were picked in February, March and April. The worker had to cut the flowers from the bulb and put them into a box. The box had to be full by the time the horse and cart returned so that the full box could be loaded onto the cart (and an empty box taken off the moving cart to be filled with more flowers). My father, being very clever, got the rest of the workers to agree that each would stop the cart once during the day so everyone got a little break from the work without anyone being sent home. I think they started at 7a.m. and finished at 5pm on weekdays and worked 8a.m. to 1p.m. on Saturdays. They were only allowed half an hour for their lunch break and, even in the worst weather, the only protection they had was to squat in the shelter of the hedgerows surrounding the field to eat their sandwiches.

One day there was a need to fertilise one of the fields. Unfortunately, there was no manure, and especially no chemical fertilisers, available for use on a field that was designated for flower production. If the intended field to be fertilised grew vegetables or fruit, then manure or artificial fertiliser would have been made available. The owner hit on a way of fertilising his field. He heard that, not far away, there was a slaughterhouse that had a heap of rotting offal, which was unfit for human or animal consumption. The farm owner bought the heap at a very cheap price, so saving the slaughterhouse from having to dispose of it. He then arranged for his workers, including Henry, to take the farm lorry to the slaughterhouse and load the rotting offal (which by then was very foul smelling) and, using just garden forks, to take it to the appropriate field and spread it (while standing on the back of the lorry as it was driven over the field). One can imagine how unpleasant the task would have been: there was a lot of it, and the field was large. Also, it was a warm sunny day. By lunchtime the workers, including my father, had loaded the last of the putrid offal on to the truck and decided that before spreading it they would stop at the local pub, where the cheapest drink was scrumpy (this is a very rough cider with a high alcoholic content). They were all feeling so wretched that they drank far too much scrumpy than was good for them, and as a result had a much longer lunch break than was normally allowed. The owner of the farm came looking for them thinking something must have happened. When he came past the pub, he not only saw but also smelled his truck outside the pub, still with the last load of offal on it. The men were sitting outside the pub, as the landlord would not allow them into the premises because they, too, smelled. When the owner saw them, he was initially furious and (being the very hard task master that he was) he told them he was going to send all the workers home there and then, without being paid for the day. He then realised that someone was going to have to drive the lorry onto the field and spread the offal. It could not be left outside the pub overnight because the landlord was becoming very angry. So, after a little while, he relented and said that if the men (once they were a little more sober) took the lorry and dumped the last load in the field and spread it then they could go home, and he would pay them for the day. This was done in the early afternoon. The plan was to plough the offal into the soil the next day. The rotting process would create carbon dioxide, which would encourage the growth of bacteria, which in turn would fertilise the field. Unfortunately, the owner had not reckoned with the sea bird population, which came by the thousands and stripped the field clean of every scrap before the light faded.

My mother, meanwhile, in October 1940 managed to get a job as a machinist in Barnstaple, nearly six miles away from Braunton. But in early March 1941, according to her Alien's Registration Certificate, she received permission to work at Sandy Lane Farm and was "authorised to possess a pedal cycle for use in connection with employment at Sandy Lane Farm, Braunton only".

Later in March, my parents move again because they both got jobs at Dartington Hall, Orchards Department, at Marley Fruit Farm near Totnes, Devon. Initially they had accommodation with a Mrs Hodge of Venton Farm, Dartington. By then my mother was about three months pregnant with my sister. Her permission to retain a pedal cycle in her possession is amended in order to travel to Marley Fruit Farm in April 1941. They both reported moving their place of work to Marley Fruit Farm, and continued to be given permission to "retain in their possession" bicycles purely for the purpose of travelling to and from their employment.

This restriction on the use of the bicycles reminded me of a story my father told me very soon after my sister was born. He or my mother saw in the "for sale" section of the local newspaper a second-hand baby pram, being offered very cheaply. But the address was some five miles from where they lived and, because my father was not allowed to use his bicycle for personal journeys, he had to walk the five miles to where the pram was for sale. Luckily, when he got there the pram had not been sold so he bought it and then had to push the pram the five miles back home.

In October 1941 my sister was born in Totnes Hospital. When my father heard the news, he went to visit my mother and, because he worked on a fruit farm, she was expecting him to bring to her (in hospital) fruit and possibly flowers. But no, he arrived with a bag of treacle toffee. At the time, sweets were in very short supply but, as it was only a month away from Bonfire Night, treacle toffee was being made and Henry managed to buy some. As he strode into the ward, my mother was disappointed to see that he was not carrying fruit or flowers. With a flourish, he threw the bag of treacle toffee on to her bed; my mother was just about to remonstrate with him when she realised how hungry she was, having not eaten since well before the birth. She picked up the paper bag and ate the toffee immediately.

A few days later she returned with the baby to their home. In those days, babies' nappies were made of a kind of towelling cloth and, having been soiled, had to be boiled — which Christine had to do in the common kitchen they shared with the lady of the house. All went well for a few weeks until the landlady began to complain that the constant boiling of the nappies (and the steam and subsequent dampness of drying them) was beginning to affect her chest. So, she told them they had to leave.

By this time, it was winter and there was little or no accommodation available for married couples with a young baby, especially with all the people in Plymouth who had been bombed out of their homes. Henry and Christine were forced to search for new lodgings. Eventually they found a derelict, condemned cottage in Dartington and moved there in early December, with winter already upon them. My mother's permission to own and use a pedal cycle was revoked, presumably because after the birth of my sister she could no longer work so there was no justification for her to have one.

As mentioned previously, a telegram arrived at the cottage telling of the fate of my grandmother Ilona; apart from this very sad incident my parents told me they were very happy there. My father had for some time been doing a correspondence course with the Royal Horticultural

Society, and in June 1942 was notified that he had passed the Society's General Examination in Horticulture. Later, and as a result of passing the examination, he was awarded by the R.H.S. a Fellowship of the society and so had the letters F.R.H.S. (Fellow of the Royal Horticultural Society) after his name.

Although very happy at Marley Fruit, Henry felt he had learned all he could and, having decided he wanted to pursue a career in horticulture, realised he had to move on to gain further experience. He took a job in Southampton at the Wilton Road Nurseries. Again because of the Aliens' Registration Regulations, he was required to inform the authorities of his new position and relocation and was subsequently given permission to reside in a "Protected Area" as an agricultural worker.

Later, he received permission from the Chief Constable "to drive a lorry, motor car and motor tractor in connection with his employment". He also received permission "to use and possess a wireless receiving set". In the November he was enrolled by the County Borough as a Fire Guard and given permission to be away from his place of residence between the hours of 10.30 p.m. and 6 a.m. The role of Fire Guard entailed him standing watch on tall buildings during bombing raids and notifying the fire service if he saw flames coming from a building.

I have only three stories from my parents' time in Southampton. The first, my mother told me. Normally she looked after my sister before she went to sleep (my sister by then was a very lively child of about two years old). My father would read or, after having received permission, he would listen to the radio. One day my mother saw there was a film playing at the local cinema that she particularly wanted to see. She told my father that she would be going out to the pictures and that he would have to bathe and then put Helen to bed. I don't know if he made the mistake of thinking a little extra play time with her father would be good for father-daughter bonding, or if she just refused to go to bed. When my mother returned from the cinema, she found my father totally exhausted and at his wits' end as to what to do with the very excited and lively child (who by now was having a whale of a time jumping all over him). He could not get her to be quiet. My mother, who was made of stronger stuff where children were concerned, picked up my sister and put her firmly into bed. The exhausted child immediately fell asleep.

The next story comes from my sister. She can remember living in a flat in Bridlington Avenue. It concerned the Morrison Shelter in the flat. She remembers sleeping in the shelter with my mother. At the time, they had a cat, and my sister wanted it to be in the shelter with them, but naturally my mother would not allow it and made the cat stay outside. This made my sister very upset, but my mother never relented.

Lastly a story from my father. When he was working at the nursery, one day he was told to fertilise the tomato plants but could not find any fertiliser. He asked someone where he could find it and the person said they did not have any fertiliser, but that they used a very natural product. The man then demonstrated how the tomatoes were fertilised, by taking a watering can and urinating into it until about a quarter full. He then diluted the urine with tap water until the can was full. The resulting solution was then poured on to the base of the tomato plants, subsequently producing an excellent crop of tomatoes.

As ever with my father, after gaining all the knowledge and experience he could from Wilton Road Nurseries he wanted to yet again further his horticultural career. He learned of a position as head gardener with a Lieutenant Colonel Wynne-Finch in North Wales. He got the job and yet again had to report to the Aliens Registration Office at the end of March 1944 that he would be changing his address and employment. My sister told me she thinks they travelled by train from Southampton to Betws-y-Coed. Once there he had to report his arrival and new employment to the local police.

My parents and sister, who was by now two-and-a-half years old, were accommodated in the lodge house. There was a Head Gardener's Cottage but the previous head gardener, a Mr Dickie (who had retired) still lived in it, so my parents had to make do with the lodge.

In early June 1945 my father reported to the Denbighshire Constabulary that he wanted to visit his distant relations (Herbert Fränkel and Herbert's mother, Adele) in London. On arrival he reported to the Metropolitan Police and on his return, he reported to the Denbighshire Police. Having not seen Herbert Fränkel and his mother since before the war, they obviously exchanged all the news of what had happened to family, friends and acquaintances.

This is probably when my father, who by then knew the fate of his parents, would have told Herbert that Sir Henry Strakosch would not provide the 200 pounds sterling as surety for his mother, Ilona, to flee to the United Kingdom. According to Mary, then the maid and later Herbert's wife, Herbert became very upset, asking why he (Henry) had not come to him for the money as he would have gladly provided it. The reason I believe Herbert would have gladly made the money available was because of the help, particularly financially, that Ilona had given his mother (Adele) after her husband Otto had died. The answer to the question as to why neither my father nor Ilona ever asked Herbert will always remain a mystery; similarly, when and where did my father ask Sir Henry Strakosch to help Ilona?

Again, my sister, father and mother have told me stories of their time in Pentrevoelas in North Wales. Having obtained permission to use a motor vehicle, my father could use the van, which was for use in connection with Voelas Hall. The first time he went to use it, another employee accompanied him. They were going to drive down to Betws-y-Coed via the main A5 road, which at that time entailed a steep and winding descent. The passenger encouraged my father to drive as quickly as possible, as there was a competition among the local drivers to see who could descend the fastest. Unfortunately, on one blind curve they met a car coming the other way on the wrong side of the road. My father swerved to avoid the car and, in doing so, drove up the grass bank, where the van performed a perfect three hundred and sixty degree roll back on to its wheels, and my father continued driving in the right direction. Suddenly he was aware of a terrible smell in the van, and then realised that his passenger had soiled himself.

The lady of the house objected to the gardeners smoking whilst at work so she complained to my father, saying that she could not understand how the British military forbid smoking while on duty whilst my father could not do the same in the gardens. Henry politely pointed out that, although Voelas Hall and Gardens was owned by a Lieutenant Colonel, it still did not put it under military jurisdiction; furthermore, it was hard enough as it was to find labour to do gardening when much better paid war work was available.

They supplemented the shortage of gardeners by using prisoners of war. My sister remembers particularly the Italian prisoners who, almost to a man, loved children and made presents for those with whom they came into contact (for example, wonderful toys that were beautifully crafted out of the simplest of materials, such as odd pieces of cloth, wood and tin cans). One prisoner called Roma always tried to make my sister laugh. On one occasion he had to burn a pile of leaves and, as it began to smoke — and before it began to burn properly, he sat on it, making her laugh out loud.

One day my father took my sister into the large glass conservatory, where a peach tree was growing on the south-facing wall, with ripe fruit hanging from it. Being wartime, with food rationing and my parents not having much money, she had never seen a peach before, never mind tasted one. It was forbidden for employees (even the head gardener, our father) to pick and eat fruit without the express permission of the owner, but nevertheless my father picked one of the peaches and gave it to Helen, who ate it. She said it tasted wonderful. When she had finished, my father took the peach stone and buried it deep in the soil of the conservatory. I often wondered if another peach tree grew in that spot.

After arriving at Voelas Hall, my parents made friends with Ruth and Dai Jones. There were probably several reasons why they became friends. Firstly, Dai was the local butcher in the village of Pentrevoelas, and during the war it was essential to be on good terms with one's butcher. That was not the only reason to be friends with Dai; he was a fun-loving person with a twinkle in his eye, whose first language was Welsh. He had a wide intellect, to which my parents could relate. A further reason was Ruth, who was a German Jew originally from Stettin. She managed to escape to England before the war and joined the Women's Land Army. She was put to work on a farm near Pentrevoelas, for several years, where she met and married Dai. Ruth was the daughter of a Jewish doctor.

Ruth told me that her parents, in attempting to avoid persecution and deportation, somehow managed to travel to the Black Forest. There, deep in the woods, they found a cabin in which they hoped to survive. Unfortunately, soon after finding the cabin and establishing a home there her father became ill and died. For obvious reasons her mother could not go to the authorities to report his death, so she dug a hole in the ground near the cabin and buried her father there. Ruth was also a highly intelligent woman, who I am sure my parents also related to because she, too, was a refugee, she was from central Europe, and she spoke German.

Ruth and Dai became lifelong friends of my parents. When I was born in 1946, they were my godparents. Many years after my parents had died, I re-established contact with them. Dai told me about the first New Year my parents celebrated in Voelas Lodge. Dai and Ruth were invited for a meal and to see in the New Year. My mother, even with food shortages and wartime rationing, managed to cook a sumptuous meal, which they ate at about seven in the evening. They then chatted, putting the world to rights, and suddenly, Dai told me, at about nine-thirty my father announced he was hungry and what could Christine quickly cook to keep him from starving to death. Dai said that he was flabbergasted that anybody could even think of food after the meal they had just eaten. He was full of admiration for my father, in that he could even consider eating again so soon. Typical of my mother, she quickly went to the kitchen and made a Pilaf from the leftovers of the dinner. Later that same evening, having seen the New Year in, my sister told me they did Bleigiessen (where one melts a small amount of lead and then drop it into cold water, creating a solid shape). The participants then have to suggest what the resulting shape represents.

A few other things of note happened while my parents and sister were in North Wales. Firstly, at some point Mr Dickie (my father's predecessor) died and, as a result, the Head Gardener's Cottage became available, and my parents and sister moved from the lodge to the cottage. Whether Mr Dickie was a bachelor or a widower is not known, but he left quite a lot of personal furniture and other belongings, which my parents either bought from his estate or just took over their ownership.

Up until now my parents had always lived in furnished accommodation and therefore, apart from personal clothing and some easily transportable items, they had not acquired very much in the way of belongings — mainly because they did not have much money. The only things I am aware they had, were the clothes and cabin trunks they had both brought to England before the war, and any clothes and other easily transportable items (such as bedding and so forth) that they had managed to purchase cheaply since their marriage.

I only became aware of some of these items from Mr. Dickie when I was four or five and we had moved away from Pentrevoelas. There was a lovely bedroom dressing table set (complete with a mirror, chairs and side tables) made from bamboo, an upholstered couch and arm chair, beds and a chest of drawers, two Windsor chairs, a gate-leg oak dining table, two upholstered straight-back dining chairs, an enamel-covered kitchen table and a silver-faced perpetual calendar (which I still have). There was enough to furnish the next two houses where we lived.

Unfortunately, after that we lived in much smaller accommodation and much of the above (including the original cabin trunks that came from both Austria and Poland) had to be stored in damp, cold, disused gardeners' accommodation known as "bothies" — where it all simply rotted away. Today some of the items of furniture would be regarded as antiques, and would be of value.

The other major event while they lived in the Head Gardener's cottage was my birth. My mother told me that a doctor and a midwife or district nurse were in attendance. When I was young, I had bright red curly hair and as I appeared out of my mother the doctor declared, "Oh, here comes a carrot top!" As my mother pushed and strained to expel me from her body, she managed to soil the bed; she was very embarrassed but the nurse said that she should not worry as it often happened. However, ever since my mother told me this, I have regarded myself as a big shit.

Perhaps the most important event of early 1946 (apart from my birth) was that a letter arrived from my mother's parents, Bianca and Adolf Blaschke. My father told me how they got the address. My mother's brother-in-law (Jupp) was in an American prisoner-of-war camp and because he had never joined the Nazi Party he worked in an office where he got to know an American. At that time, so soon after the war, Germans were not allowed to send letters outside the country. The American was going to the UK and Jupp asked him to take a letter to England and post it there. The letter was written by my mother's parents to the last address they had from Christine, in Devon, because that was the last time my mother sent them a twenty-five word Red Cross message. My father told me it was only by sheer luck that the letter reached my mother at all. He told me it was re-addressed several times after leaving Devon and took months to reach them in Pentrevoelas (my father having left a forwarding address every time they moved). Unfortunately, this letter to my mother has not survived.

Only two other letters from my mother's parents to her have survived. They are mainly concerned with information of a personal nature, but towards the end of the second letter Adolf writes the following: "Terrible events are taking place in our dear homeland [Upper Silesia]. Hitler has created a terrible hate which will be avenged on us a hundredfold. The German people have been burdened with a disgrace and shame that will still not be forgotten by the end of the century." I am not sure whether Adolf meant some form of physical, economic or financial vengeance. Certainly, the Russians took many people from that region to Siberia who never returned, and they confiscated a large amount of moveable assets that were also transported to the then Soviet Union.

At least the United States of America created the Marshall Plan, which helped to finance and restart many industries in countries such as West Germany and Austria. But he was right in one respect: Germany will be forever reminded of what happened as a result of the Holocaust, not only to the Jews but also to the gypsies, homosexuals and people who were mentally ill.

My father, having been brought up in very formal upper Viennese society, wrote to Adolf Blaschke sometime in 1946 asking for Christine's hand in marriage; although Christine and Henry had been married for nearly six years he explained his background and his profession (so my mother told me). I have no idea if Adolf replied and, if so, what the content of his letter was.

As always with my father, he was anxious to progress in his chosen profession and when a position became available as manager of a plant nursery owned by the Co-operative Wholesale Society (CWS) in Warburton near Lymn, Cheshire, he applied for and got the job in late May. For whatever reason it took a while for the Frank family to move to Warburton, but they eventually did in early August.

The furniture from the Head Gardener's Cottage was loaded into a removal van. Now — something I should have mentioned earlier — at some stage during their stay at Voelas, Henry began keeping bees because the honey would have been a welcome addition in those days of strict rationing. The other reason was that a beekeeper could apply for and obtain an extra ration of sugar for the bees. In my father's case about half the additional sugar ration quickly found its way directly on to the family table, the bees having to go hungry in the winter.

When it came time to move, the bees were put in a special box with fine wire mesh on the sides so they could not escape, and the empty beehives and the special box were loaded with family possessions into the removal van. Dai, who had a car, agreed to take my father, mother, sister and me to Warburton — following the furniture van all the way to what was to be our first home there, Gate House Farm.

During the journey it became clear that there was a hole in the box containing the bees and because the furniture van had no doors at the back (just a tarpaulin) the bees began to appear outside the back of the van. Because the Queen was still in the box the bees did not fly away but continued to follow the van, which would not have travelled at a very fast speed in those days. When the van and the family arrived at Gate House Farm the general manager for the area was waiting to greet them.

My father quickly jumped out of the car to warn him of the danger of the bees, explaining what must have happened. The general manager assured my father that there was no problem because he himself was an expert beekeeper who had no fear of them, and therefore would climb into the van, retrieve the special box and set it on the ground away from the van so that unloading could begin (and the bees not in the box could settle on it to be near the Queen). With a flourish the general manager pulled back the tarpaulin and, without any protection, attempted to climb into the van, when an angry bee stung him on the very tip of his nose. What happened after that I don't know but the family moved in and settled down to life in Warburton.

My sister, who was five years old on 5th October 1946, began her schooling in Warburton. As the distance from Gatehouse Farm was too long for her to walk, our father took her to Altrincham and bought her an old children's "sit up and beg"-type bicycle. He then taught her to ride it and asked a couple of the neighbouring boys if she could ride with them to school each day, to which they agreed — thus enabling Helen to go to school.

Gatehouse Farm was not only where we lived when we first arrived in Warburton but also the administration office for the CWS in the area. CWS not only owned the plant nursery but also several farms. The man in charge of the office was a Mr Clark.

When my father arrived in Warburton the only telephone available was in the office, which was some way from the nursery. So, if my father needed to use a telephone for business purposes he had to walk or cycle to the office. The telephone system was not automatic, one had to lift the receiver and wait for the operator to come on the line and ask to whom and to where one wanted to be connected. One day he had to call a nursery in a place called Lower Peover pronounced Peeva. My father did not know this so, on hearing the operator's voice, he pronounced it phonetically in his Austrian-accented English, asking for Lower Pee Over. Mr Clark fell off his chair laughing.

In early December we moved from Gatehouse Farm to Lane End Farm, which I remember. It was a typical brick-built cottage with a barn attached on one side of the house. If I remember correctly, downstairs there was a kitchen, a living room and a sitting room that was normally only used when we had visitors. Upstairs we had three bedrooms and a bathroom. The toilet was outside near the barn and consisted of a wooden board with a hole in it, under which was a large tin bucket that was emptied once a week by the council.

Chapter 5

Early post War Years: Warburton, Cheshire, England

The winter of 1946-47 was one of the coldest winters on record. A farmer who remembered the winter told me there were many weeks of frost and during that time he could not get a plough in the ground. Up until the late 1960s most British homes were heated by open coal fires, which are a very inefficient form of domestic heating. Coal heaps at the railheads in towns and cities, and in power stations and factories, froze. It required enormous amounts of labour to break it up so that it could be burned — even soldiers had to be deployed to help.

My first memory probably happened in 1947 while my mother took me out for a walk in the pram. All I can remember is my mother wearing what my sister later told me was a red pony-skin coat, which she probably brought with her from Poland.

The only other thing of note is that both Henry and Christine became naturalized British citizens in December. As a result, they were no longer required to report to the police whenever they moved house and therefore their Certificates of Registration ceased to be used. Interestingly, both documents were cancelled in June 1945 after World War II had ended but continued to be used until Henry and Christine were naturalised.

Both Christine and Henry were very proud of their British citizenship. They both had a good command of the English language but spoke it with central European accents, which made them easy to identify as foreigners. People often said to them, "Oh, you're not English are you?", to which my mother or father would reply, "No, I came from [either Austria or Poland depending on whether it as my father or mother who was talking] before the war and I was naturalised in 1947. England is my home and I have no wish to return to where I was born."

It must have been a relief for them to be naturalised. They often talked about what would happen to them, particularly in the early part of the war, if Germany invaded the United Kingdom. This was a particular worry to my father because he had been registered as a Jew in Austria and would have suffered at the hands of the German invaders.

It was also a worry for my mother because if my father had been incarcerated in a concentration camp, she too would have been persecuted for marrying a Jew. As the war progressed, they must have been concerned about what would happen to them once the war ended. Would my father be sent back to Vienna with my mother and sister? Would the Russians, who by that time were occupying parts of Vienna, discover my mother was Polish and send her and possibly my sister to Poland?

In July 1948 my mother travelled to Nuremburg, Germany, to see her parents for the first time in nine-and-a-half years. She travelled by train and the journey took two days. When she arrived in Nuremburg, she nearly missed her parents, who had driven from Allesberg to meet her. Grandfather Blaschke describes (in a further addition to his "Niederschrift") how Christine spent ten days in their (and her sister Waldtraut's) company.

My mother was horrified by the destruction caused by bombing in Nuremburg. She also told me that the trains on which she travelled were in poor repair, often with windows boarded-up because the glass was broken or missing completely, and how British and American troops constantly patrolled the trains asking (in very aggressive tones) for identity papers; when she presented her British passport they were taken aback and, having inspected it, always handed it to her with a salute and a smile.

I can remember very little of 1949 except for the visit of Evy von Seeman to my parents in Warburton, Cheshire. It was a Sunday and my mother prepared her usual excellent British Sunday lunch. This little lady arrived in a car and brought me, as a toy, a red London double-decker bus, which with my typical spoilt carelessness I managed to lose some years later. I know it was a Sunday because usually Sunday afternoons were the only time our father had time to play with us which, as always, I was looking forward to immensely.

Many years later Evy told me that after lunch she and my father retired to the sitting room where the fire was lit, and they sat down to talk about what had happened in the intervening years since they had seen each other. Evy said she became very annoyed with me because I would not leave my father alone and kept asking him to play with me. Evy had been brought up in a time and social class where children were to be seen but not heard.

Another memory I have is that we went on holiday to Golden Sands Holiday Camp in Rhyl, North Wales. I was still only three-and-a-quarter years old and did not understand the concept of holidays. We went for a week. All our clothes and food for the week were packed into one of the cabin trunks that my parents had brought to England in 1939.

We were due to travel by train from Warburton station; it probably no longer exists. The station was some way from our house — a walk of over a mile or more. In order to transport the large and heavy cabin trunk to the station my father borrowed a hand cart from the nursery, giving instructions to one of his workers (who lived near the station) to take it back to the nursery on the Monday.

Later, whenever my mother and father were having an argument (particularly over money) my mother would remind my father that he had been too mean to order a taxi to take us to the station and that it had embarrassed her to have to walk with the cabin trunk on the handcart. My father would reply saying that they did not have the money to afford a taxi and that there were no taxis to be had in Warburton.

I was still too little to walk so I was put in my pushchair with my mother pushing me, my sister walking along beside her and my father pushing the handcart. On arrival at the station my father hoisted the cabin trunk up onto his shoulder and we walked on to the platform.

When the train arrived, we all got in and sat down; soon after I felt I needed the toilet and began to fidget. My mother asked me if I wanted to go to the toilet. By this time the train had briefly stopped at a couple of stations and I thought going to the toilet would mean getting off the train at a station, very quickly going to the toilet, and hopefully getting back on the train before it left. I was terrified that, if I were too slow, I would be left watching the train leave the station.

After even more desperate fidgeting my mother took me firmly by the hand and said we were going to the toilet. I screamed in fear at the thought of being left alone on the station platform as the train pulled out without me. But as I was pulled down the corridor my mother opened a door in the carriage and there was a toilet and washbasin. To my great relief, pleasure and interest I discovered one could go to the toilet on the train — and while it was moving. If only someone had told me beforehand.

The holiday camp consisted of small wooden chalets, each with a veranda. I was too young to remember what other amenities were available — probably communal washing and toilet facilities at least. Judging by the photographs, the chalets were situated close to the beach and similarly the weather appears to have been very pleasant.

The only thing I can clearly remember during our stay was that one day my sister and father were not there, only my mother. She told me that they had gone somewhere together and said that, as long as I did not go far, I could go out on my own. This for me (at the age of three) was the opportunity for a big adventure, so out I went.

Not far from the chalet (towards the beach) there was a man with a camera who asked if he could take my photograph. He stood me on a concrete block, saying that I should stand up straight, and then he took my picture. Then he gave me a card with his address on it, telling me that I should give this to my parents and if they sent it to him with a postal order for a small amount of money, he would send them the picture of me that he had taken.

I ran back to my mother and gave her the card. Soon after my father and sister returned, my father (having read the card) decided that he would send it accompanied by the required postal order. Sometime later the photograph arrived at our home in Warburton.

The last memory I have is of me riding a tricycle along the front path at our house in Lane End Farm. At that time, my mother kept chickens to supplement the egg ration. I was wearing long trousers. The tricycle had no chain guard and suddenly I noticed my right foot would not move and I realised my trouser leg was caught between the chain and the sprocket.

At first, I was unconcerned, thinking only of how I might free myself, but then along came one of the chickens and it began pecking me. I screamed in terror; fortunately, the kitchen window looked on to the drive and my mother (who was working there at the time) heard my screams, came running out and shooed the chicken away, extricated my trouser leg and carried me (still screaming in terror) into the house. I am sure she pacified me with something sweet. Since that moment I am terrified to pick up any feathered bird and cannot eat an egg where I can see the yolk and white separately (either boiled, fried, poached or scrambled).

One Sunday afternoon as we were finishing our lunch there was a knock on the door and I was sent to open it (because I had just reached sufficient height that by standing on tip toe and stretching my arm up high, I could open the door). Outside stood a man and a woman: he had dark hair and she was blonde. The woman said, in a foreign accent, "Hello, is your mummy and daddy in?" I ran back to my parents and told them there was someone at the door who wanted to speak to them.

My father went to the door and spoke to them. They had quite a long conversation. I can't remember if he invited them in or not or whether my mother joined in the conversation. I do remember the man, who was simply called Power, never appeared again.

Next time the woman, called Ursal, originally from Hamburg, appeared she came with a man called Jaro, who was from Czechoslovakia. Both were refugees. I never learned why Ursal had come to England but Jaro had been conscripted into the German army and, as he told me the last time I met him, in 1998, he had been captured by the Americans and spent several years as a prisoner-of-war in America.

When he was released, he was due to be transported back to Czechoslovakia, which by then was in the hands of the Communist Government. He travelled by ship to the United Kingdom and was then due to be transported by rail to Harwich, across the North Sea by ferry and on by rail to his hometown of Pilsen (or Budweis). Somehow, he managed to convince the authorities that he would be incarcerated if he returned behind the Iron Curtain. Hence, he was released in England.

How he met Ursal I don't know. The only thing I can remember is that Ursal at that time worked as a cook at the local American Air Force base called Burton Wood. He was a mechanic and they arrived on his motorbike. Helen and I were very impressed with the motorbike — so much so that he took Helen, first, on the pillion for a ride and then, because I was still quite small, he sat me on the petrol tank and took me for a more sedentary ride. I was over the moon, especially as being in front of the rider I could see where I was going, unlike Helen who had to lean on his back, put her arms around his waist and have her hair streaming out behind her.

Ursal and Jaro married and moved to a place called Pickmere near Northwich in Cheshire. They remained good friends with my parents throughout their lives. My father often helped them and other people originally from central and eastern Europe with British bureaucracy, such as obtaining British citizenship and tax returns. In return Jaro would help my father with various mechanical problems at the nursery, such as repairing and refurbishing pumps.

When I last met them in 1998, I had already moved to Austria and married Ellie. We visited them in Pickmere. Jaro had been a British citizen for a long while but he still regarded himself as Austrian. He had been born in Pilsen (or Budweis) in 1916, when Czechoslovakia was still part of the Austro-Hungarian Empire. Under the law of the blood in Latin, "Jus Sanguinis", he was technically correct.

I asked Ursal how she came to knock on our door all those years ago in 1949. She said she had heard there was a German-speaking couple living in a house in Warburton so she and Power cycled from Burton Wood and asked around and were directed to our house.

Lastly, Ursal introduced my parents to another German-speaking woman who worked as a cleaner at the American base. Her name was Tessa. She was small and thin with a very flamboyant attitude in the way she spoke, dressed and smoked. I remember her bright red lipstick. According to my mother or father she was the illegitimate child of an Austro-Hungarian nobleman.

During the war she made her way to Paris, where she was a dancer. Tessa once told us that late at night in Paris, when travelling by the Metro, one had to stand near the wall. The French would let the occupying German forces stand at the edge of the platform and as a train came into the station the French would surge forward as a crowd and push at least one German soldier in front of an on-coming train.

She somehow managed to get my mother and myself invited to the base and entertained to coffee by a General's wife at her home. We arrived and were shown to a very up-market prefab. Inside was a very gracious American lady, who had Tessa serve the coffee to my mother and herself.

The only thing that I remember was that the General's wife said she made an absolute rule that her coffee and tea services — from the pots to the cream and milk jugs, sugar bowls and spoons — were made out of solid silver. I remember her saying, "I won't have any plate in the house." I thought to myself, I wonder what they eat from if they don't have any plates in the house.

Tessa visited us several times. On one of the first occasions, my mother had invited the wife of my father's area manager to tea. They got into conversation about beauty treatments. At that time, just after the war, cosmetics were in very short supply. Tessa, being a very vivacious and plausible person, explained how she had learned to use various natural products as beauty treatments.

The wife of the area manager became very interested and Tessa suggested that she could administer her treatments to her while she (Tessa) was staying with my parents. The woman agreed and a date in the very near future was set. My mother, always looking for ways to supplement the family's income while remaining at home with her children, became excited at the prospect of her and Tessa setting up in business together.

The appointed day came and the woman arrived. She had previously asked for her face and feet to be treated. The morning before the lady was due to arrive (in the afternoon), my mother (under Tessa's supervision) had made up a mixture of egg yolk, grated carrots, flour and lemon juice as a face-and-feet pack (and also slices of peeled cucumber for the eyes).

I remember the lady being sat in a chair and her face and feet washed, and then the mixture was applied liberally, and the cucumber slices placed on her eyes. The woman had to remain still for quite a long period of time, and I was told to play quietly so as she would not be disturbed. Then the moment came when the cucumber slices were removed from her eyes and the face-and-feet pack washed or scraped away.

To the absolute horror of my mother the lady's face and feet had turned bright orange. About this time my father returned home from work expecting to meet the very beautiful and satisfied wife of his boss. But my mother pushed him into the kitchen and explained what had happened as Tessa tried to reduce the brightness of the orange stain in the lady's skin by rubbing-in more lemon juice.

My father was very angry and distressed. He told my mother that he would lose his job and they would probably be sued in the courts and pay damages. I don't know what actually happened but I believe the orange stain did eventually disappear, my father did not lose his job and they were not sued for damages. My father absolutely forbade my mother to be involved in any more money-making schemes.

One evening while Tessa was staying with us my parents took her to a pub in Dunham Massey called the Vine. It had a piano and Tessa sat down at the piano and began to play. The pub was full and because Tessa was such an accomplished pianist everyone stopped talking and listened when they heard her play. The last time we heard from Tessa was in the late 1950s or early 1960s. She had returned to Austria or Hungary and said she would love to visit us if only we would send her the money.

My sister, during a school trip, contracted food poisoning and had to remain in bed for about two weeks in order to recover. Unfortunately, the people in the village had organised a trip to the circus during her confinement. My parents realised that Helen was too ill to go to the circus so it was decided that our mother would stay at home with Helen and my father would take me to the circus.

I must have still been fairly young - maybe three or four. The place where the bus (that was to take everybody) was parked was some distance away. So, my father put me in the push-chair as I was too young for the long walk. It must have been winter as I remember my father wearing his dark blue double-breasted Crombie coat that he had brought with him from Vienna.

How I knew the coat had come from Vienna was because in January 1969 I was sent to Moscow on a business trip. In order to have something warm to wear my father lent me this coat.

Going back to the circus trip, I remember that he, like my mother, had no Sunday-best clothes, so even his most presentable ones were quite shabby or old-fashioned, but once he put the coat on, he looked very impressive. I can remember my father pushing me to the bus and him wearing the coat.

Apart from that I can't really remember anything about where we went to see the circus or the journey there and back. However, I can remember thinking that when Helen went anywhere, she could describe it in great detail, making it sound very interesting. I was always jealous of her ability to be so articulate. So, being the horrible child I was, I had no concern for her lying in bed ill and having missed the circus. My only thought was how I could make her jealous. I had recently learned what for me was a big word, and that word was "special".

Immediately we arrived home I was allowed to go up to Helen, lying in bed, and tell her what a wonderful time I had had. Of course, she asked me to describe the circus, but being such a mean, and inarticulate child, I just told her it was a "special circus". She asked me what I meant by this but of course I had no clue what I meant. I could not just describe to her the animals and acts I had seen. To make her jealous all I kept saying was that it was a "special circus".

Years later when we talked about this incident, she asked me what I meant. At least I had the good grace to explain that I was jealous of her ability to describe and articulate, and the only way I had of getting at her was to say the circus was special.

At about this time, while still not old enough to attend school, I can remember Sikhs and Africans coming to the door with suitcases full of cleaning materials and nylons. They would walk for miles trying to sell their wares. My mother always bought something from them, be it a pack of yellow dusters or sometimes, if she could afford it, nylons.

Normally she did not have money for the luxury of nylons so she would buy a bottle of light brown liquid and rub it on her legs and then draw with a black pencil a line down the back of her legs, so that it looked like she was wearing stockings.

Once, I saw a man with a moustache riding a bicycle wearing a beret. Draped around his neck and bike were strings of onions. I asked my father who he was. My father explained that this man had come from France to sell his onions. For many years I always thought that, having crossed the channel by ferry, he had ridden all the way from Dover to

Warburton in Cheshire. Only much later did it dawn on me that he would have taken the train, or that a group of them came on a lorry then spread out around the countryside.

It was probably in late summer or early autumn 1949 when my father bought his first car. Actually, he bought two cars — the Austin 16 saloon and an Austin 16 Tourer with a fold-down hood. Both were built some time in the middle 1930s. The tourer was not in working order and was stored under a tarpaulin. My father had converted his Austrian driving licence into a UK one. Our mother had let her Polish driving licence lapse and so had to take the UK driving test, which she proudly told everyone she passed first time.

By that time, they would have been aware that Adolf and Bianca Blaschke were planning to arrive for Christmas 1949. I think they were beginning to realise that Lane End Farm had no modern conveniences. There was only an outside toilet and the bath in the bathroom was not enamelled (and the metal it was made from was rusty in places). My mother had tried painting it with emulsion paint, but the paint fell away from the metal and lay in large flakes at the bottom.

My father saw an advert for a head gardener's job near Halifax or Huddersfield and so one Saturday or Sunday we drove over to see the garden and the accommodation being offered. The house was newly-built, with all modern conveniences. My father was offered the position so he and my mother decided that he should take the job.

Tendering his resignation to the CWS caused consternation among the management because in three years he had made a success of the nursery. They asked why he was leaving and he replied that it was because of the substandard accommodation in which he and his family were living.

It was quickly agreed that if he would rescind his resignation the CWS would undertake certain renovations immediately. As a result, an inside toilet and a new bath and washbasin were installed. Also, one or two other things were done.

In the front garden there was a cesspit into which ran the wastewater from the kitchen and bathroom. This was the obvious place to direct the waste from the new inside toilet, as the house was not connected to a mains sewage system. One day during the renovations a large tanker truck arrived with long, wide-diameter flexible pipes that, having been attached to a pump on the back of the truck, were lowered into the pit so that the collected waste could be sucked out. As a result of the above renovations we remained in Warburton for a further three-and-a-half years.

In January 1950 grandfather and grandmother Blaschke arrived in Warburton. They should have come earlier and been with us for Christmas 1949 but my grandfather had to have an operation and they therefore delayed their visit until he had recovered. My mother told me later that when they arrived my grandfather still looked very poorly from his operation so my father took out life insurance on my grandfather so that they could bury him if he died!

My parents were very poor. My father earned less than eight pounds per week as manager of the CWS nursery, and although he often had to work long hours, he, unlike the workers on the nursery, received no payment for overtime. Food was still scarce and rationed in 1949 and 1950, and my parents were very worried about how they would feed us and my grandparents (as their planned visit was due to last six months).

We lived in a cottage that had been a farm in former days and that still had a pigsty, so my father bought a couple of piglets (we named them Daisy and Rosy), put them in the sty and fed them until my grandparents arrived. My parents then had the pigs slaughtered by our local butcher and probably came to some kind of arrangement with him that the meat could be stored in the butcher's cold room (as we, of course, had no fridge or freezer).

Also, there were no carpets in the house and except for a couple of rugs there were just bare rough floorboards and red tiles in the kitchen. My mother came up with the idea of buying rolls of roofing felt, laying it down wall-to-wall on the wooden floors and painting it bright green (with remarkable effect).

My grandparents' journey to England entailed travelling from Nuremburg by train to one of the channel ports (or Hook of Holland) and then by boat to England and by train to London, where my father met them because they spoke no English. They all had to stay overnight in the Victoria Station Hotel in London before completing their journey by bus to us in Cheshire. They arrived at our home after I was put to bed, so

I did not see them until the next morning when I was introduced to a very kind old lady, my grandmother, and the rather stern and foreboding figure of my grandfather.

The first thing I remember was that I could not understand what they were saying because they spoke German and I spoke English. Although my parents were both native German speakers my father forbade the speaking of German to my sister and myself because he was concerned of the reaction we would receive so soon after the war if, as a family, we spoke German in the street. My grandparents were bitterly disappointed and as a result I was never able to speak to them.

I can't remember much about their visit. Soon after they arrived my mother decided, for the first time in a long time, that she would go shopping on her own in our local town, Altrincham, as she could leave me in the care of her parents. She naturally wanted to have a bit of freedom.

I only noticed that she was going as she was walking out of the door. I was in my socks and at that time still could not tie my own shoelaces, so I pulled on my wellingtons but on the wrong feet. As I tried to run after her I fell in the road and as she got on the bus I lay there crying. My grandparents picked me up and took me back into the house, where my sobbing continued. Grandmother sat me on her knee and began to bounce a ball back and forth to grandfather; this naturally fascinated me to the extent that my crying stopped and I was happy.

Another time, my mother took her parents and myself shopping to Manchester. I remember we visited the two big department stores, Lewis' and Kendal Milne. Both had escalators as well as lifts and I was frightened, being so young, of getting off and on the escalators. So, my grandmother and grandfather took my hands and lifted me on and off, which I thoroughly enjoyed.

They had been with us for just over a month when my grandmother had her 71st birthday on 23rd February 1950. My mother had prepared food but during the party my grandmother began to feel unwell. It was thought that it was indigestion from having eaten too much rich food so she went to bed to rest, where she remained until the doctor was called the next day. He examined her and declared that she had cardiac thrombosis.

She died four days later on 28th February, hence the reason she is buried in the graveyard of the Old Warburton Church. My grandfather was very distressed but decided to remain in England with us until his planned return in August.

My parents were so poor they had to borrow the money to pay for the funeral. Presumably my grandfather repaid them at a later date. He certainly sent a traditional central European wooden cross, which had a round metal cover to protect it from the weather (they are often seen in German and Austrian graveyards). Unfortunately, it was vandalised many years later and, before her death, my mother had a granite gravestone erected, which still stands today.

The Austin saloon allowed my parents to take my grandfather on day-trips into Cheshire and Derbyshire and to some flower shows. It also allowed them to take us all, including my grandfather, on holiday in the summer to Llandudno (a resort town on the North Wales coast) for a week.

My parents decided that my grandfather could not face the return journey to Germany alone so it was decided that my aunt Waldtraut, whom I did not know existed, would come to England and accompany him home. So, one evening in August we went by car to Warrington station to collect her. She naturally spoke German with my parents and her father; I turned to my sister and said that I could not understand what was being said and she replied, "They are speaking German and we don't speak it." There began my total unwillingness to ever learn a foreign language. until I finally settled in Austria in November 1997 — where I had to learn to speak German to survive.

The next day my aunt offered to cook and prepared a soup of chicken broth with fine noodles. I had never seen chicken noodle soup in my short life, so I took one look at it and asked my sister what it was. She whispered, "Don't eat the soup, it is full of white worms." Of course, me being the stubborn, spoilt child that I was, I refused to eat it and my parents were mortified when I blurted out that Helen had told me that the soup had white worms in it. I suppose coming from Central and Eastern Europe they were looking forward to enjoying a traditional dish of their youth but I spoilt it all with my outburst. Waldtraut and Grandfather Blaschke left for Germany on 28th August 1950.

Chapter 6

Food, Popular Culture, English Friends and Initial Success

I once asked my father about food rationing and what was available during the war. He explained that early on in the war meat was very scarce —even tinned meat such as spam and corned beef. After a short while, American tinned meat began to appear in the shops and this was spiced (as he and my mother remembered before they came to England). They, of course, thoroughly enjoyed it. However, the British were not accustomed to such flavours and began to complain, and as a result the Americans sent bland un-spiced tinned meat instead.

On a more general point, as I write I realise what a culture shock it must have been for my parents — coming from Central and Eastern Europe — to live and become accustomed to the food, climate and customs of what was a very traditional non-multicultural England in the late 1930s, 1940s and 1950s.

When I was young the boys around me would talk of football and cricket and what their fathers thought about various teams and players. My parents almost never talked about sport except occasionally about when they themselves had sailed, swum, skied, played tennis or climbed and hiked. These were not the leisure activities of the working class in which I grew up.

My father read the political parts of the newspaper but rarely the sports pages. My mother was an avid reader, as I have said previously, of the Readers Digest and religiously completed the News of the World crossword on a Sunday. Similarly, when my mother and father discussed the social activities in which they had been involved, these were very different to my friends' parents — where the father went to the pub and played darts or cards and the mothers were involved in the Women's Institute or Mothers' Union.

News and entertainment reached our home via an old, black Bakelite valve wireless. It had a round cream-coloured gauze face, where the sound came from, two knobs (one for on and off and volume, the other for station selection). Between the two controls there was a small glass panel with names such as "Light" and "Home" and then capital cities such as "Paris, Berlin, Vienna, Warsaw etc."

My father listened mainly to the evening news, followed (because he was a nurseryman) by the weather. My mother religiously followed Mrs Dale's Diary, the daily life of a doctor's wife, and my sister followed the Archers. I had no real interest. Sometimes I would sit and listen with my mother to "Listen with Mother" and "Woman's Hour" but in both cases I often became bored and went off to play.

On Sunday, as we were having lunch, we listened to "Two-way Family Favourites", the programme that allowed families and loved ones in the UK to request songs and music for British military personnel stationed abroad, and vice versa. This was followed by the cries of "Wakey Wakey" as the "Billy Cotton Band Show" began. My mother's favourite song was "Don't Fence Me In" and mine was "The Yellow Rose of Texas".

Our newspapers at the time were the "The News Chronicle" and on Sunday, ostensibly so my mother could do the crossword, "The News of the World", both now defunct. Magazines included "Woman" or "Woman's Own", periodicals the "Reader's Digest" and, for Helen and myself the "Beano" and "Dandy" comics. These last two were upgraded, for me, to "The Eagle" (I loved the adventures of Dan Dare and his sidekick Digby) and the "Girl" for Helen. Finally, there was the monthly periodical from the Royal Horticultural Society that, like "The News Chronicle", our father read. The RHS publications were kept in order to refer to a particular article, if necessary. Occasionally Aunty Trautel would send my parents German magazines. The only one I can remember is "Der Stern". My parents would read them avidly as a link to their pasts.

In 1951 or 1952 a family we knew in Warburton bought a television. They invited us to watch it with them one evening. The picture was in black and white, four hundred and five lines of transmission and a tiny nine-inch screen. The picture appeared quite blurred to my eyes, and my father said later it gave him a headache. Whatever we watched bored me:

it was either a man playing classical music on a piano or some woman dancing. I decided television was not for me. How wrong I was.

As I have already mentioned, my parents were poor. A further example of how poor they were at that time was when a fellow manager of a nearby nursery asked my father to bring the family to Sunday afternoon tea. My mother suddenly realised she had no Sunday-best clothes. She worried about this for a few days. She had a presentable skirt but no blouse to go with it. Then with a flash of inspiration she took some fine hessian from the nursery, dyed it orange, wrapped it around her shoulders and pinned it down the front like a stole.

When the nursery manager's wife died, in 1987 or 1988, I attended the funeral and afterwards, while talking to him about times gone by, he recounted the story of my mother coming to tea wearing dyed hessian. Until my parents died, they remained friends with the couple and they would visit each other from time to time, both in England and in Spain. As a footnote to this story the lady who died was the same one that visited when my mother's friend Joachim, from before the war, surprisingly called one Sunday afternoon in 1965.

In order to have an interest outside of the home my mother joined the local amateur dramatic group; she loved it. It was good fun and very absorbing, at the same time, as she had to learn her lines and her movements on the stage. According to my sister Helen she was in two plays. I can remember one, which required a female cast member to speak with a continental European accent. Of course, our mother was absolutely suited to the part. She threw herself into it with great gusto. I remember we were allowed to see the matinee performance and, although I could not understand what was going on, I was very impressed at seeing my mother on stage. Helen told me that either in that play or the other one, in the last scene our mother had to kiss a male cast member on the lips.

Sometime in autumn 1950 my parents made friends with John and Edith Aird, who lived in Penketh, a suburb of Warrington. They had no children of their own so spoiled Helen and myself. Before Christmas 1950 we visited them at their home and, as we were leaving, they gave Helen and me five shillings each — in those days an absolute fortune but today worth only twenty-five pence.

Helen had saved her pocket money to buy Christmas presents so she already had five shillings, making the princely sum of ten shillings. I had squandered my pocket money on sweets. It was decided that Helen and I would be allowed to take the bus together into Altrincham to buy Christmas presents.

My mother was worried that I would not have enough money with which to buy presents, so she offered me a ten shilling note in exchange for the five shillings I had been given, making the excuse she needed the change for some reason. I was very reluctant to make the exchange because I had two large half-crown coins and she was offering me a piece of red paper in exchange. Finally, after much cajoling from Helen and my mother, I accepted but was still not sure I had done the right thing.

Once in Altrincham Helen took me to Woolworths, which had the cheapest presents. I bought a large bottle of very cheap scent for my mother and a packet of aerogram letters for my father. I can't remember if I bought anything for Helen or any of my friends. I probably kept the rest of the money for myself. Helen diligently bought thoughtful presents for our parents, her friends and me.

A few days later it was Christmas and our parents always kept the Central and Eastern European custom of giving us our presents on the evening of Christmas Eve, following a meal (which was never Turkey as that was reserved for our traditional British Christmas Day lunch). After the meal our parents would go into the sitting room where they had put up the Christmas tree and decorated it. They lit real candles and our wrapped presents were put under the tree. When ready they would ring a little bell and we would enter to see this fairyland spectacle. It was a wonder to behold. With the meal we had Christmas crackers and in the crackers were paper hats, which Helen and I would put on.

This particular year Helen decided she would take her hat off and put the presents she had to give in the hat and carry them into the room. I decided to do the same, with disastrous consequences. The large glass bottle of very cheap perfume was too heavy for the thin paper hat and as I was about to run into the room full of joy the bag burst, and the bottle of perfume crashed onto the tiled floor and smashed. Of course, I cried and spoilt the whole event for everyone.

My mother gathered me in her arms and said it didn't matter and told me to give the pack of aerogram letters to my father, which I did but I could not be consoled — what was meant to be my crowning moment ended in great disappointment. My mother fetched a brush and dustpan and a mop and bucket, and as she cleared up said that the perfume had a lovely strong smell and it would remain in the house for some time.

Several years later, when we were laughing about the incident, she admitted to me she had been pleased about what had happened because the perfume was so strong, and the smell was not to her liking, she would never have used it. About the same time my father asked me to fetch some item from his personal drawer. In it I found the pack of aerogrammes unopened. I asked him why he had never used them and he explained because they were not franked — that is, a post office stamp was not printed on them so if he had used them he would have had to put a stamp on, which would have taken the weight over the airmail letter rate.

A further story about my mother and perfume relates to a Bruno Shadek, a Viennise man who also had to escape Nazism because of his Jewish background. My father met him when they both worked for Mr Ball in Devon in 1939 and 1940. My father and Bruno became lifelong friends because they both came from Vienna.

Bruno spent Christmas with them every year; this continued even when my parents moved to Cheshire and Bruno was in London and then when he moved to the Isle of Wight. He would usually arrive late on Christmas Eve and leave on Boxing Day because he could only leave work at 5pm on 24th December and had to be back at work on the morning of the 27th.

He was a bachelor who always bought presents for all of us. My mother would write to him in September inviting him, and he would reply confirming he was coming and asking what we all wanted as a Christmas present. My mother would write again with a list of our wishes.

One year my mother asked him to bring for her a bottle very expensive Arpege perfume. Bruno did not earn much money so when giving out his presents he gave my mother a tiny bottle of it. Still she was thrilled and began to open it while standing up and she dropped it, breaking the neck off the bottle. She quickly picked it up but had lost some of the contents. She stood it on the mantle shelf of the fireplace saying she would put it in another container once she had seen everyone else open their presents. The fire was lit and the room was warm and when she returned to the broken bottle nearly all the remains of the perfume had evaporated. The last drops she put behind her ears.

The last Christmas Bruno came was in 1966 and he did not seem himself. He was very quiet and dosed a lot. My parents asked him if he was well, to which he replied that he was. He left as usual in late afternoon on Boxing Day, to be at work the following day. A few weeks later my parents received a call from the Isle of Wight police saying he had not reported for work one morning and that his colleagues had gone to where he lived but got no answer at his door. The police were called and they broke down the door to find him lying on the floor, having died some time earlier. Looking through his things the only address they found was that of my parents. He appeared to have no other friends or relatives. My father informed the police that he did have a male cousin going by the same surname, who lived in Cyprus, and that they should contact him.

I remember the Airds gave Helen and myself a toothbrush each. The handles of the brushes were moulded into the shape of the Disney characters Donald Duck and Mini Mouse. Naturally Helen, being the girl, got the Mini Mouse shape and I the Donald Duck one. We were totally enthralled by these and on the way home in the car that evening we were talking about nothing else but brushing our teeth with them before we went to bed.

On reaching home my mother told us she would save the big moment of brushing our teeth with our new toothbrushes until the morning, as it would be a nice way to start the day. She also said that instead of brushing our teeth in the bathroom upstairs as usual she would allow us to perform this part of our ablutions immediately after breakfast in the kitchen. Seeing this as a good idea I went to bed tired but excited that the next morning I would be brushing my teeth with Donald Duck. I accept that it was not the top dog (Mickey Mouse) but it was very close.

Next morning, I awoke totally beside myself with excitement. I rushed downstairs to have breakfast and saw both toothbrushes in our tooth mugs (plastic beakers actually) in water on the windowsill in front of the kitchen sink. I ate my breakfast dreaming of Donald Duck and how I would tell my friends about this momentous occasion, and how I would be looked up to and admired for having a Donald Duck toothbrush. With breakfast finished our mother asked us to brush our teeth at the kitchen sink.

The moment had finally arrived for me to achieve my crowning glory. I arose from the table and walked towards the kitchen sink, and at that moment my mother said, "stop, wait, I have to change the water in the beakers." Our mother, ever protective of us, had filled the beakers with boiling hot water and put the toothbrushes into the hot water in order to sterilise them. Of course, the plastic of the beakers and the toothbrushes were not heat-resistant. The beakers (Helen's was pink and mine was blue) were quite misshapen and from then on totally unusable.

The Donald Duck toothbrush was twisted and buckled out of all recognition. The functioning end of the brush was twisted like a bottle brush or narrow-bore pipe brush. But even worse was that Donald himself was now bent and deformed like some strange medieval gargoyle. I cried and cried and could not be consoled; Helen was obviously disappointed but accepted her lot. But the pain and devastation: my whole world had completely collapsed. I had no great story to tell my friends and nothing to boast about.

My father, who had still not gone to work, was furious with our mother, asking how could she put boiling water into cheap plastic beakers and similarly immerse the toothbrushes. Did she not realise what would happen? — she had wasted the cost of the beakers and the toothbrushes, and caused terrible devastation to her children. My mother, stoic as always, just shrugged her shoulders and got on with it. She told us to go upstairs with a couple of old cups and to brush our teeth with our usual toothbrushes. Crestfallen, I mounted the stairs.

During the war the nursery my father now managed had been used for the production of food, in the form of vegetables and fruit, as had most nurseries and also private gardens. With the end of the war and military personnel being de-mobilised, the general public wanted some return to normality. So, on arrival at Warburton Nursery my father realised that people would now be wanting not only to grow vegetables and fruit but also flowers in their gardens, and to have them in their homes. So, he mainly moved the production away from fruit and vegetables to annuals, herbaceous and cut flowers, all of them being in demand in the retail and wholesale trade. Within the herbaceous group he also included Alpine plants, maybe because of where he came from, but also in a small garden it would be possible to create a very attractive rock garden.

It all proved to be a great success, not only because of his capability as a gardener but also because the nursery was owned by the Co-operative Wholesale Society (CWS), which had an enormous sales and distribution network all over the country, so the plants could be sold through the huge number of Co-op shops and to other nurseries.

Orders from CWS sales representatives, countrywide Co-op distribution centres and other nurseries and shops would either be telephoned or arrived by post during the day (until early afternoon). The workforce would then go into the fields and glasshouses and begin to collect the plants and flowers for all the orders. They would be brought to what seemed to me an enormous packing shed, where they were divided up into individual orders and packed in cardboard boxes, addressed and labelled. All the packages were then put onto a red, electrically-propelled hand truck with battery and taken to the railway station for dispatch all over the country.

A worker would supposedly walk with the truck because its road tax registration classification did not allow the person operating it to ride on it. However, my father once told me the local policeman was forever complaining to him that he had seen one of the workers riding on the truck.

One day my father came home with a wheelbarrow containing some large rocks and Alpine plants. He cut away a small corner of the back lawn and, in what seemed like a few minutes, created a rock garden that he said was to be mine and that I had to look after. I was fascinated by it but being so young and spoilt I soon lost interest and left my father to care for it.

As I said above, he mainly moved production away from fruit and vegetables but not completely. My sister Helen confirmed to me that there was at least one small field where raspberries, red currants and gooseberries were harvested at the appropriate time. Two fields further away from the nursery, near Gate House Farm, were used to grow strawberries. I can only remember the plants lying on, and surrounded by, straw and full of fruit.

My sister told me that in 1950 he had a bumper crop of strawberries that ripened at more or less the same time. He had limited permanent labour and certainly not enough to harvest the crop before the birds ate it or it spoiled. So, he put the word about — asking in particular local housewives and others if they wanted to work on a piece-rate basis of so many old pence per small basket (known locally as a punnet). Some women did respond but he realised he still did not have enough labour. Luckily the spring half-term school holiday was about to begin the following week, so he went to the local school and asked if there were children over the age of seven who would like to earn some money. Sufficient children responded positively, and the harvest began on the Saturday.

Both my mother and Helen joined in but I was too young. Before starting on the first day my father explained the system to the pickers. They would each be given one or two large baskets, depending on whether they were an adult or a child, and they would be allocated rows to pick and put the fruit into the baskets; Once the baskets were full they had to take them into a barn, where the strawberries were put into individual punnets, and in doing so they were checked to ensure that the fruit was of the correct quality. The punnets were then weighed to ensure each contained the same weight of fruit. Lastly, he told them they could eat all the strawberries they wanted while working but they could not take any home. Helen told me she can remember one day earning half a crown — now twelve-and-a-half pence, but then a princely sum for a child. After a couple of days, the pickers stopped eating the strawberries because they had had their fill. It was a very successful harvest.

Because several housewives (such as my mother) had young children they had to accompany them, as most did not or could not afford to have anyone look after their children. We young children knew each other and played together on the edge of the field. We were not allowed to walk down the rows of strawberries for fear of treading on them. One of the two fields was across the road from Gate House Farm and, when our mothers had filled their baskets, we would often accompany them over the road to the barn where the strawberries were checked and weighed.

I remember standing by my mother, ready to cross, when a big boy with a flat workingman's cap came riding out of the farm on his bicycle, carrying two large baskets full of strawberries. As he raced away my father came running out on to the road to try and stop him, calling after him that he was a thief (having stolen the full baskets). I remember thinking what could I do to try and stop him? I picked up a small stone and tried to throw it at him, but it fell well short of him and he rode away with his booty.

As young children we became bored just playing together at the edge of the field. Fortunately for me, one woman who had two young sons had her old mother-in-law at home. So, it was suggested that the old woman could look after the three of us for the day. I was delighted because it meant I could play at their house with their toys and also out in their garden.

We played all morning then began to realise we were hungry, so we went inside to see what the boys' grandmother had made us for lunch. She appeared to me to be a very old woman; she was always dressed in black, probably widow's-weeds, and sat in a chair by the fire.

When we went inside to ask what was for lunch, she looked nonplussed and then suddenly said, "Would you all like sugar butties?" (a butty is, or was, the Cheshire or North of England dialect word for a sandwich). She went into the kitchen, took some slices of white bread and spread margarine on to them. Now, I hated the taste of margarine — it was not like the modern-day vegetable spreads. I was not looking forward to my lunch at all until I saw that she liberally sprinkled sugar over the margarine and folded the slice of bread to make a sandwich. I bit into it. It tasted delicious — the sugar made the bright yellow, grease-like, post-war, revolting margarine appear totally different to the palate. I wolfed it down, hoping for another, but there was only sufficient bread, margarine and sugar for us to have one each because the rest, she explained, was needed for the family's evening meal.

Later in the afternoon my mother came to collect me and as we walked home, she asked if I had had any lunch. With great enthusiasm I described the magnificent feast I had eaten. She was horrified and for the rest of the harvest insisted I accompany her during the day, so she could ensure I was given some wholesome sandwiches (which she had made). That was the only time in my life I can remember eating a sugar butty and I still pine for one today.

For my birthday in 1951 I was given a magnificent toy tractor. It was green in colour. I had visited a boy called Edward who lived in Warburton. His father was a relatively well-off farmer and every time he bought a new tractor (and he had several at the time) Edward received a model of it. Edward showed me his collection and, as he was a very generous and caring boy, he let me play with them.

Knowing my birthday was coming, my parents asked me what I wanted as a present. The answer was obvious — a toy tractor — and although it in no way matched Edward's collection of dye-cast models I was very proud of it. It was only made of thin metal and, unlike Edward's, the steering wheel did not turn the front wheels and the engine was painted on the metal.

Now that I was five my mother decided I should walk to the Sunday morning church service with my sister Helen and the three children from across the road. All the way to church I kept talking about my tractor to the extent that all the others told me not to be so boastful. Actually, in true northern or Cheshire English, they called me a "show-off".

It was the church service just before Easter and we sung the hymn "There is a Green Hill far away", after which the vicar gave his sermon. We were sat in the front row of pews. I listened for a few moments and realised the vicar was talking about the Green Hill in the hymn. Naturally, to enhance his sermon and support his endeavours in explaining the significance of the Green Hill, I shouted out "Canon Gravel —", for that was his title and name, "I have a Green Tractor." To which he replied, directly to me, without missing a beat, "Oh have you? How nice, I must come and see it" and continued on with his sermon.

I sat there feeling very smug and pleased with myself as to how I had so helpfully contributed to his sermon, absolutely sure that the rest of the congregation would now understand that not only can hills be green but also tractors, and the congregation now knew that I had a green toy tractor and therefore soon the whole village would know. I must admit there was some snickering from my sister and the other three children but I assumed they were just jealous that it was I, the youngest of us, who had made such a significant contribution to the sermon.

At home my sister Helen told our parents and one them said that it was rude to interrupt the vicar, which I accepted, but they did not scold me and I went off to play with my beloved tractor. Years later, when talking about this incident, my sister said that when I made my utterance, she and the other three children were so embarrassed they just wished the whole world would have opened up and swallowed them.

After Easter I started at the village school in Warburton. There were two classes, two rooms and two teachers — a Mrs Lewis, the head teacher, and a Miss Longhurst. The larger room was for the five-to-seven-year-olds, known as "infants" and taught by Mrs Lewis; the smaller room held the eight-to-eleven-year-olds, known as "the top class" but actually the primary school class, taught by Miss Longhurst. Assembly was held in the large room, where the whole school prayed and sang a hymn before beginning lessons.

I can't remember much about the first day except we were all given an exercise book, which held blank pages. Mrs Lewis asked us to come up to her desk at the front, one at a time, where she wrote our names on the front cover. She then turned to the first blank page and drew two perfect small trees, then a "plus" sign and asked, "If one was to draw another tree just the same how many trees would there be in total?" She said we should show the answer as a number of trees, as we did not know our numbers at that point.

I knew the answer so went back to my place and tried to draw the three trees as perfectly as she had drawn the other two but could not do it. I kept trying and trying but they all came out as odd shapes. By the time she called time I still had not done it, and so from then on, she saw me as a slow and lazy idiot. I then noticed other children had very quickly drawn three circles to represent the leaves and branches, each one attached to a line pointing downwards, which represented the trunk.

When Mrs Lewis began teaching multiplication tables they made no sense to me and in exasperation she dragged me from my little table and chair and marched me into a small storage room, where she gave me the tables she had written out and said I was to stay there until I had learned them. I was crying and very distressed, not knowing what to do.

I began reading them out loud, over and over again. Suddenly I noticed I was not looking at the piece of paper but had learned them by rote. So, when she came to see how I was getting on and asked me a couple of multiplications I answered them perfectly. She was very surprised and reluctantly allowed me to re-join the class. Since that day multiplication tables (to the twelve times) have never been a problem.

In late April we received a parcel from Aunt Waldtraut; in it were various gifts for my mother, father, sister and me. My gift was a pair of short leather trousers, called "Lederhosen" in German. My mother saw these as a godsend as I was growing quickly and I was rough and careless with my clothes. The "Lederhosen" were one or two sizes too big and because they were made from leather were virtually indestructible. This saved my parents from having to buy me new short trousers frequently, and my mother from having to repair my cloth trousers as regularly.

The most peculiar thing about the "Lederhosen" was that there was no button fly (where today there would be a zip). Instead the trousers had just one button at the waist, leaving the rest open. To protect one's modesty there was a wide flap of leather at the bottom of the fly that reached up to the waist, and there were two button-holes at the top edges of the flap, which attached to the buttons, thus keeping things out of sight. Going to the toilet, the other boys made fun of me, as I had to undo both buttons and let the flap dangle. But that was not the worst problem: when one leaned forward the flap bulged showing gaps at either side big enough to allow curious little girls of my age to slide their hands in and ask, "What's in there?" It tickled. Some of the girls thought that it was a muff where one could put one's hands on cold days.

Chapter 7

The First Great Adventure and London

In the summer of 1951 we, as a family, embarked on a great adventure. For some time, my father, John Aird and the father of our friends who lived across the road had been working in their spare time on the renovation of the Austin 16 Tourer (which had remained under a tarpaulin in the barn). Apparently, its engine was in better condition than the saloon version, which at that time was our family car. Mainly they exchanged parts that were in better condition on the saloon with poorer parts on the Tourer. Also, the saloon had a problem in that the half-shafts broke with alarming regularity. My father scoured scrapyards looking for Austin 16 half-shafts, and the spare half-shafts were a permanent feature in the boot. Mother once told us that she and my father became so expert at changing half-shafts they could do it in an hour.

The only bit of the renovation I can remember was that the Tourer was jacked up on to blocks of wood and the wheels were removed. To give an idea of the age of the car, the wheels were not the solid metal ones of today but had spokes. I was warned on pain of death not to climb into the car because I might disturb the blocks such that the car would fall from them, causing damage in the process. One day my mother said to me, "Come and look in the sitting room, the wheels have come back from being sandblasted." Of course, I had no idea what sandblasted meant — I thought perhaps they had been taken to the seaside. On entering the front room, I saw the wheels, painted with aluminium paint, looking absolutely pristine. I thought they would look fabulous in that colour on the car. A day or so later they had disappeared from the living room and I rushed round to the barn expecting to see the aluminium-painted wheels on the car, but they were not there. A few days later my mother told me once again to go into the sitting room and there were the wheels but this time painted black. I was so disappointed that they had been painted a boring black, the same as the bodywork of the car. I had not realised, and in fact did not know at that time, that the aluminium paint was only a primer.

My father and the others continued to work in the evenings and weekends on the Tourer. Then one day it was gone and a few days later the saloon had also disappeared. Suddenly the Tourer reappeared with a new hood and this was now our family car. The saloon never returned and I learned later that it had been sold — partly to pay for the major renovations of the Tourer, and the rest to pay for part of our great summer adventure. Suddenly one Friday, as Helen and I finished school for the summer holidays, my mother was frantically packing and after our family meal in the evening my father disappeared with the car once more. We were put to bed and woken early the next morning, washed, dressed and given breakfast.

My father told me sometime later that even on the night before our departure there was still quite a lot of work to be done on the car. John Aird, who had trained as a mechanic, knew someone in Penketh who had a workshop where the remaining work could be accomplished. As they worked on the car it became apparent that more and more things still had to be done. Finally, in the early hours of the Saturday morning, they thought they had done everything and then suddenly, while the car was still over the pit, someone noticed that much of the exhaust pipe was very badly rusted and was in imminent danger of falling off. Fortunately, lying in the workshop was a long piece of steel tubing with a bend at one end. It was exactly the right diameter to fit into the remaining piece of non-rusted exhaust pipe that led up to the engine manifold.

At about 4.30 in the morning it seemed the car was ready, when it was realised the car didn't have any side windows. Unlike the saloon there were no wind-up-and-down side windows fitted into the doors. Judging by the holes in the top of the doors and in the underside supports of the folding cloth roof, the car had obviously been fitted with some form of removable windows, which had become mislaid over time. Although the hood would protect the passengers from rain falling straight down when stationary, when in motion the passengers would be soaked. Fortunately, someone found some strips of wood and clear plastic and quickly made temporary windows that could be fitted when it rained.

These having been made, my father drove away from the workshop and arrived home at about 6.00 in the morning. He climbed into a hot bath, in which he had a few minutes sleep. Then, looking somewhat bleary-eyed, he put our luggage in the boot, the house door was locked and our neighbours from across the road came to wave us off.

We drove to Penketh where the Airds lived. They put their luggage in the boot. It was then realised that there was only seating for five people. With my father and John Aird in the front and my mother, Helen and Edith Aird on the back seat, there was no place for me. The thought of me — a large, lively five-year-old — sitting on someone's lap was not to be tolerated. So, John or Edith ran back into their house and came out with a tiny stool, which fitted perfectly over the prop-shaft tunnel, and we drove away. Although I am sure my mother or father had previously told me, I had no idea or concept of where we were going except that the Airds, whom I liked because they often gave me money and sweets, were accompanying us.

Our great adventure was now beginning. The plan was to drive to Dover, take the overnight ferry to Dunkirk, then drive to Hamburg to visit Aunt Waldtraut, Uncle Jupp and our cousins Karl-Heinz, Brigitte and Hildegard. After staying in Hamburg, we would drive to Allesberg, south of Nuremburg, to visit Grandfather Blaschke. Finally, we would drive on to St. Gilgen in Austria to meet up with Aunt Evy and Uncle Peter Seemann. The latter were actually some form of cousins of my father.

These were the days before motorways in Britain, so I have very little idea of the route we took except that we drove through or near Oxford — where the heavens opened and we encountered flooding. I was quite frightened by the situation and the hastily made side windows gave no protection against the powerful rain.

All I can remember is that when the water became so high on the road, John Aird got out of the car and turned the exhaust pipe so that the bend at the end (which had been pointing downwards) now pointed upwards. Only much later in life did I realise that he had done this to lessen the risk of the engine sucking in floodwater and so damaging it beyond repair.

By now John was driving and although a mechanic by trade he had become a chauffeur to the managing director of a firm, which often meant driving to London. At some point I fell asleep. The next thing I can remember was being carried into what seemed to be a building with potted plants in the corridors, then through a narrow door and being laid down on a bunk bed. We were in fact on the St. Germain car ferry's maiden voyage from Dover to Dunkirk — hence all the pot plants.

I woke in the morning to the most horrific sight. It was first-light and the boat was not moving; it was, in fact, already tied up alongside a quay. As I looked out of the porthole into the harbour, I saw sunken ships where only the funnel was above water. Others were either on their sides or completely capsized.

Looking towards what had been the town, most buildings had been totally or partially destroyed and even the ones that still appeared complete had holes in their roofs or in the walls. There was rubble everywhere. I had seen bombsites when my parents took us to Manchester or Liverpool but they were just spaces between buildings, used as car parks; here was total devastation. I was absolutely terrified but my parents appeared to be in a hurry to disembark so I, for once, just did what I was told and didn't scream and cry as was my normal wont.

The St. Germain, although very new, was not like modern car ferries with bow and stern doors that enabled a roll-on-roll-off facility. The car was on the deck but under cover. We all climbed into the car and drove down a curved ramp to the quay. As we were about to leave the harbour area, I saw this red-and-white pole blocking our path. My father got out of the car and gave a man in a uniform a large folder, which I later learned included the adults' passports and a carnet (the car's passport). A few minutes later my father got back into the car and the man in the uniform lifted the red-and-white pole by pushing downwards on the end, to which a weight was attached.

As we drove off, my mother told me the pole was a border post and we had just entered France. What or who was France, I thought? Driving through the town, the road was clear of rubble but it was piled up in heaps at the side of the road. The shops, such as they were, consisted of wooden shacks with little windows. There were very few people about because it was so early and the whole place had a very eerie feeling.

We drove to Brussels. I only know this because my father showed us all the small statue of the boy urinating. It made me laugh. I can't remember anything more about that day except that it was perhaps cold and wet and the side screens had been abandoned (because at speeds over about twenty miles per hour their poor construction meant they blew inwards and provided no protection whatsoever).

The next thing I remember was being in Hamburg and being introduced to my Uncle Jupp and cousins Karl-Heinz, Brigitte and Hildegard (of course I had already met Aunt Waldtraut). I can't remember much about our time in Hamburg except perhaps on the first afternoon my mother told me we were going to have "Torte". I asked what that was and she told me it meant cake. I was very pleased. The only other thing I remember was that we went to the seaside to a place called Cuxhaven, which had a nice sandy beach and big double-seat high-backed wicker chairs.

I can't remember leaving Hamburg but the next morning I woke up in a strange bed next to a little girl in a cot (who was speaking to me but I could not understand a word). I tried to ask her where I was but she obviously could not understand me either. Tears began to well up as I thought my parents had decided to leave me there.

Then I thought I must be brave and accept my new life in this strange country. I began to wonder where I would go to school, if one day I would be able to learn German and who my new parents were and what they would be like. I was thinking about my toys that I had left behind in England, and would my new parents provide me with some with which to play.

Just as I had accepted my lot, mother walked in holding a little girl. "Ah," I thought, "she has decided to swap me for her and my mother has come to say goodbye." All of a sudden, she said I had to get up and dress, as we were due to leave shortly. So, I would be going with them. I was so happy. I have no idea who the family we stayed with were. I suspect they were known to my mother and had agreed to put us up for the night.

We drove on in the direction of Allesberg, a small village south of Nuremburg where my grandfather lived. I don't remember if we had another overnight stop but I remember us driving on the Autobahn, which was more-or-less devoid of other traffic except for heavy goods vehicles with trailers (such as I had not seen before) and Allied troop convoys.

Once, it began to rain and the hood was down so we stopped under a bridge and as John Aird and my father were putting up the hood a siren sounded. John said he thought someone was coming to get us. This absolutely terrified me because I imagined being separated from my mother, father and sister forever. It turned out John was just having a joke.

Whenever we needed to stay overnight, we would arrive in a small town or village and ask a local person where we could find a cheap and clean place to stay. One evening as we drove into a village there was a policeman directing the traffic. My mother was driving at the time and my father said, "Ask the policeman." My mother, having been waved through, was travelling at probably twenty miles per hour. She braked but the cables had stretched and hence the brakes were not very effective. The car was so old it did not have hydraulic brakes. We went sailing past the policeman and eventually we came to a stop. My father was shouting at my mother to drive on before the policeman spotted our faulty brakes but my mother did not do so. She reversed up to the policeman and asked his advice as to where to stay for the night.

One night we came to a "Gasthaus" and the landlord advised us to put the car in the barn for safekeeping. As I got out, I noticed wooden boxes with holes in them, fixed to the wall at my height. I immediately put my hand in one and to my amazement felt a cold wet pig's snout. I shouted with surprise and my father or mother explained that the pigsty was on the other side of the wall, and in very cold or wet weather the pigs could be fed from inside the barn. My parents loved the simple "Gasthaus" food, for example dumplings with "Sauerkraut" and pork. My sister and I refused to eat it. We had discovered Frankfurters and Coca-Cola so we had that as our meal every evening. One night the "Gasthaus" only had a local German brand of cola called "Afri-Kola"; it was nowhere near as good as the Coca-Cola and for years to come Helen and I spoke of the experience of having to drink it.

Other experiences occurred during our travels. When my mother was driving, she came up fast behind a man on a bicycle who had a bunch of flowers clipped to the carrier on the back of his bicycle. The flowers must have been ready to fall because as she overtook him the disturbed air sucked all the flower-heads away, leaving the poor man with the stems. Somewhere, I suspect in Austria, my father discovered a very smelly cheese that he had particularly enjoyed in his youth. It was small and round and wrapped in silver paper. He bought it in a shop where we had stopped for petrol. As he unwrapped it the smell, even in an open car with the roof down, was appalling. It reminded the rest of us of very sweaty feet. My father ate the cheese with relish but after so many complaints he had to throw the remains away. Interestingly, I told Ellie, my Austrian wife, this story and she could remember the cheese from her childhood and the accompanying smell.

I cannot remember arriving in Allesberg or where we stayed when we were there. My only memory is of Grandfather Blaschke's housekeeper, a Frau Wally Fiegel, taking Helen and myself for a walk through a corn field where the corn had already been cut and bundled into sheaves, and three or four of these were stood together, vertically, leaning on one another like a Red Indian tepee. At some point Wally and Helen climbed inside one but I was too scared to do so. I am sure we spent time with my grandfather but I have no recollection of it at all.

We left Allesberg and headed for St. Gilgen in Austria. St. Gilgen is situated at the west end of Lake Wolfgang, known in German as the "Wolfgangsee". Mozart's mother was born there. I can't remember if we managed to drive there in one day or not but I do remember en route we stopped at a lakeside restaurant where there were lots of wasps, of which I was terrified, and our meal was served on the most fascinating plates I had ever seen in my young life. They were oblong in shape; until then the only plates I had ever seen were round ones. The plates were divided into several compartments, into which various components of one's meal were put so that the meat, vegetables, salad, and sauces were all separate. Why such a memory has remained with me for so long I can only assume is because of my eternal love of food.

On arrival in St Gilgen, Evy Seemann told me much later, we stopped at wherever she was staying and she came running out to meet us and saw the old open car and six people climbing out of it. She thought there were so many people in the one car that it would never finish emptying.

My father was delighted to meet most of his remaining relatives again. I can remember we were taken sailing on Peter Seemann's sailing boat and my father wore white trousers, white shirt and white plimsolls for the event.

Soon after we arrived my parents bought me an Austrian Janke (a thick traditional woollen jacket) and a pair of brown leather boots; they also bought traditional Austrian clothes for Helen and themselves. One day it was decided that we were going to climb a mountain. I thought that with my Lederhosen, given to me by my aunt Waldtraut, and my Austrian Janke I would make the perfect mountain climber and when I returned home to Warburton, I would be able to boast of having climbed a big Austrian mountain.

As the moment arrived for us to depart on the expedition, I was told that Evy, my father and Helen would be going but because I was so young, I would have to stay behind with my mother. I cried, I screamed, I threw myself on the floor in temper — all to no avail. We were in the garden of the Gasthaus where we were staying and there were several people sitting having refreshments. They all looked at me but this did not deter me.

The climbing party departed and at some time my mother managed to calm me down, probably by offering me something sweet. The plan was for the climbers to walk from the Gasthaus and climb the mountain and then descend by another route. John and Edith Aird, and my mother and I, would drive to the point where the climbing party's decent met the road some way away.

The final act of pacification was that I was allowed to sit in the front seat next to the driver. When we met the intrepid group, I was able to boast to Helen that I had sat in the front seat. She told me that the path they had taken was very slippery and our father or Evy had fallen and got their hands dirty. This dissuaded me from climbing mountains for the next ten years.

I mentioned in an earlier chapter that after leaving school my father got a job in Enns in Upper Austria, which is just over the border from Lower Austria. While working there he had a girlfriend and for some reason, for which I have no explanation, when he was forced to leave

Enns in 1938 and return to his parents in Vienna, he left with this girlfriend a large, valuable ormolu clock.

I assume he had previously written to the woman explaining that he was coming to Austria and would like to visit her and retrieve the clock. So, on one of the days we were in St. Gilgen my parents drove to Enns and when they arrived the woman invited them into her home, and there was the clock in pride of place in the living room.

I don't know what actually transpired but my father much later told me my mother and the woman did not exactly hit it off, and a scene ensued with my mother wanting to take the clock and leave. My father, always fearful of the customs duty, suddenly declared that the woman should keep the clock. She appeared very pleased at having got one over on my mother. My parents left without the clock. My mother was furious and upbraided my father on what was then quite a long drive on normal roads back to St. Gilgen.

Whenever my parents were having an argument in the future, and my mother thought she was about to lose, she would bring up the matter of the clock. My father would immediately counter by saying that they would have had to pay a lot of customs duty, for which they didn't have the money. My mother, the inveterate smuggler, would further counter by saying, "Rubbish, I would have sat on the back seat with the clock hidden under my skirt so no one would have ever noticed it!" As an afterthought, I imagined the situation that it was a chiming clock that had been wound-up and that as we had driven through customs and been asked if we had anything to declare and said "No", the clock would have chimed "Bong Bong Bong."

Years later my father and I were discussing the Iron Curtain and he said, "Well, I showed you the barbed wire and watch towers at the border between Upper Austria and Lower Austria when we went to Enns in 1951." At that time the Iron Curtain went through Austria along the border between Upper Austria and Lower Austria. I said that I could not remember the occasion because I was too young.

Even later still I mentioned to Evy Seemann that my father had shown me the Iron Curtain but that I could not remember it. She replied that that was because I was not there. She went on to say that on the day our parents drove to Enns it was agreed that Evy would take Helen and myself to Bad Ischl, where there was a very famous "Konditorei" or "Patisserie" (in English a café) where, among other things, very tempting cakes are served.

She took us in her little car. I have no recollection of this either. Evy said that when we arrived at the café, she asked us what we would like to eat. Unlike in post war austerity Britain, there was a wide selection of delicious pastries and cakes available but Helen and I just gave our standard response in our northern English accents "Coca-Cola and Frankfurters please."

Several years later, when talking to my father about what had happened to his pre-war sailing boat, Swift, he explained that after the war he had written to the boatyard where it had been stored. They replied that because it had been the property of a Jewish person it had been confiscated and sailed and maintained in good condition throughout the war by a Nazi. The boat was still in the boatyard.

After the war, all confiscated property had to be returned to its rightful owners. Obviously, he could not bring it back to England so he decided to sell it. He found a buyer and sold it for five thousand Austrian Schillings. I have no idea what that was worth in UK pounds at that time, so I asked Ellie and she thought that the exchange rate at that time was about sixty Austrian Schillings to one UK pound. If that were the case Henry Frank would have received about eighty-three pounds, quite a sum in 1951.

I asked my father how he used the money. He said, "Well for a start by the time we had reached St. Gilgen we had almost run out of money, so we used some of it to get us home!" That was typical of the devil-may-care attitude of my parents at that time.

They drove all the way to St. Gilgen via London, Dover, Brussels, Hamburg and Allesberg (a journey of probably two thousand miles) on a wing-and-a-prayer that, although they would be almost out of money by the time they reached St. Gilgen, they would sell the boat and have money to get home (a journey of a further one thousand miles and several overnight stops). What if Henry had been unable to sell the boat? We could have all been living in St. Gilgen to this day. Some of the rest of the money presumably went on buying the Austrian clothes.

When I visited St. Gilgen in summer 1997 with Ellie, for the first time since 1951. Evy and Peter Seemann were there, and Peter pointed out that my father's boat, Swift, was on a mooring on the Wolfgangsee, obviously still being sailed.

I can't remember what route we took home through continental Europe or how long it took, or if we stayed overnight. I have only one memory as we approached the channel port, presumably Dunkirk again: a ship's siren sounded and John Aird, who was driving, said, "Oh, that is our ship leaving." I of course, being so young, believed him and became worried that we would have to live in the terrible bombed-out town and port of Dunkirk, which I described earlier, for the rest of our lives.

Our return ferry was not on the St. Germain so the car had to stand on the open deck during the overnight crossing, which had been quite rough and wet. As a result, the electrical leads to the spark plugs had become soaked to the extent that the car would not start as we tried to disembark in Dover. Trying to use the starter soon flattened the battery so either John Aird or my father tried to use the starting handle, but all to no avail.

At this point some of the crew decided the car would have to be pushed down the ramp, as all the other cars had already left and the ship had to sail again. So, we all got in the car and the crew pushed us to the ramp, where it rolled down at an ever-increasing pace. John Aird was in the driver's seat and at some point, he engaged a gear and let out the clutch and fortunately the engine roared into life.

Many years later, with my own family and first wife, we had borrowed a car in which the starter motor had a habit of jamming. This happened as we were attempting to disembark from the Isle of Arran ferry at Brodick. My then-wife was quite dismayed but having remembered the incident from the Dunkirk ferry in 1951 I just told the ferry crew of our problem and asked them to push us off the boat. Again, as the car gathered speed, I selected a gear and slipped the clutch and the engine roared into life and off we went.

I can't remember anything of the rest of the school holidays but when school started again, we all had to explain what we had done over the long school summer holiday. Fortunately it was in school assembly so my sister Helen was there and she was able to explain the journey and that, as my mother had told her and she often repeated for years to come, "We drove in our car through continental Europe for three weeks and did over three thousand miles."

In February 1952 King George VI died. I am sure there was a national outpouring of grief but I can't remember it. The only thing I do remember is that on the day of the funeral, at a particular time, the school radio was switched on and we all had to stand silent for three minutes when told to do so by the radio announcer. I was terrified that I would move or say something and get into trouble but I managed to stay still and quiet for the whole time, a difficult thing to do for a five-year-old.

About that time, I saw boys in the school playground playing football and when I tried to join in, I found I was clumsy and uncoordinated. Much later in life, when I was fifty-nine, I was tested for dyslexia in order to continue my Open University degree. The psychologist who conducted the test said that he thought I suffered from a mild combination of apraxia and dyslexia. My own elementary research suggests dysgraphia, particularly hand-eye coordination, seems to be closer to the symptoms I experience. None of this, to my knowledge, was known about in the early 1950s. Only when I went for my Grammar School interview in 1957 did the headmaster allude to some very early research on the topic.

Returning to my desire to play football with the other boys, I decided that what I needed were football boots and a proper football and that that would resolve all my problems. I would be ready for the big-time, very quickly scoring goals and being the team's hero. For my birthday in March I asked my parents for both the boots and the ball. They were dubious because money was tight, possibly because of the previous year's holiday. However, when my birthday came along there at the end of the bed were both boots and ball. I was over the moon.

The boots were made of unpolished rough leather, with studs made from round slices of leather nailed to the sole. The ball had an inner rubber bladder and an outer cover of pieces of oblong-shaped leather sewn together, just like the real thing I had seen in newspapers and magazines. I thought, "Now I will show the other boys, who is the best player in the school."

Sadly, it did nothing for my game or ability. I only learned later in life the proverb "A poor workman always blames his tools." In my case it was more like an incapable player blames his equipment. I played with a couple of friends a few times but I found the boots hard to walk in if I walked on a hard surface like the road. Fortunately, at six years old I began to grow quite quickly to the enormous size I am today and so soon out-grew the boots. The bladder in the ball burst. Eventually the leather outer, having been left in a damp place, became covered in mould and rotted away.

Many years later, my son went through a similar phase. We bought him football boots, probably for his sixth or seventh birthday, and that night when I went to say goodnight he was smiling very broadly. I discovered he was wearing his boots in bed!

When I first went to Warburton School the playground was just hard earth, with the odd very obstinate weed growing around the edges. When it rained it could become a sea of mud and in winter the water lying on the ground froze. Older children would run on to the ice and slide along, polishing it even further.

Some time, probably in spring 1952, workmen arrived and began to dig out and level the playground, filling it with gravel and then asphalting it. Before it was asphalted the area was bordered with long, thin kerbstones made of moulded cement. When we were sent out to play, we were expressly forbidden to stand or walk on the freshly asphalted areas but could go on to the gravel still awaiting tarmac. Even these areas had already been edged with the kerbstones.

Some of the children began standing on the stones and jumping on to the gravel area so I obviously joined in. Being bigger, or perhaps the stone I selected to jump from was not properly set in the ground, as I pushed off with my feet the stone was pushed backwards and out of line with others.

All the other children were horrified at what I had done and to save their own skins immediately went and told Mrs Lewis the headmistress. She came into the playground and immediately began to admonish me, so severely that I began to cry. The other children looked on, thankful that I was getting all the blame as Mrs Lewis questioned why I, alone, had been jumping over the stones, saying that I was to blame for the damage and that I must be punished (which meant being spanked on my backside with a plimsoll).

My world was collapsing and I was terrified about what was about to happen to me when my beloved sister spoke up and said I was not the only one who had been jumping off the stones. At this point Mrs Lewis realised it was not fair to punish me alone and, as she could not identify the other perpetrators, she told us all not to do it again and walked back into the school. When we had finished our break, a workman came and reset the stone in a few minutes.

The couple mentioned earlier (when my mother had to dye and pin hessian as a blouse in order to go to tea at their house) moved with their family of three children to Bromley, which was then in the County of Kent. It is just south of London and is now a suburb of the metropolis.

They invited us to stay with them in the summer of 1952 for a week. Because money was in short supply my parents made it our summer holiday. We drove in the Austin 16 Tourer. It was a very long journey because there were no motorways at that time, but eventually we arrived. While there I learned to ride a small bicycle on the lawn, but was so shy that I made everyone watch through the window as I rode.

I remember we visited London, saw Tower Bridge, the Tower and the Crown Jewels and finally the British Museum, but by that time I was very bored so stayed outside with my mother while the others went inside. My father, who loved classical culture, was enthralled with the exhibits. He took Helen to the National Portrait Gallery and that instilled in her a love of art, which existed within her to the day she died.

The next day we drove to Brighton. I was told I would be able to play on the beach. I imagined my father building sandcastles for me and me pouring water into the moat. I was so disappointed when I discovered that it was a pebble beach that hurt when you walked on it barefoot. Also, because it was fairly steep, I as a young child could not just run into the water and jump in the waves, yet another of my many disappointments in life.

Some of the rest of the summer holiday were spent playing with the children across the road. We would go on expeditions across the fields. We could see what appeared to us to be in the far-off distance a grass mound, so decided one morning to head off to explore. When we finally reached our goal, we saw that it was just a pile of grass sods. Nevertheless, we were happy that we had conquered yet another landmark and returned home happy in time for lunch.

Then my father said that, as I had learned to ride a bicycle while in Bromley, I could now use Helen's "sit up and beg" bicycle as she had outgrown it. Somehow in the few weeks since we had been in Bromley I had completely forgotten how to ride, so one evening my father taught me again.

He did this by taking me a little way up the lane that ran by the side of our house, sitting me on the bike and holding on to the back of the seat as he pushed me along with my feet on the pedals. As I gathered speed, he ran behind me and at some point, he let go. I blithely continued on down the lane unaware that he was no longer behind me.

As I reached the point where the lane met the main road I looked behind and saw that he was no longer there. I crossed the main road because he had not shown me how to use the brakes. There were no brakes on the little bicycle I had ridden on the lawn in Bromley. Fortunately, there was no traffic and I came to a rather painful halt in the neighbour's holly hedge, with my father running up to me asking why had I not used the brakes, and was I all right. He then extricated me, together with the bicycle, from the hedge and proceeded to teach me how to use the brakes!

From then on, I could ride a bike with increasing confidence. I began to ride along the lane, which rose to a slight crest and then dipped downwards to where it forked. One day I managed to ride over the crest and was very excited as I gathered speed on the downwards slope. All went well until I came to the fork, where there was loose gravel. I turned to take the right-fork but the front tyre lost its grip and I came off, sliding along in short trousers on the gravel. Finally, I came to a stop and saw that my right knee was bleeding profusely.

Crying and sobbing, I struggled to my feet, picked up the bicycle and hobbled home. My mother was horrified. She washed my wounds and took me to the district nurse, who bandaged my right leg from my thigh down to my calf, telling my mother to wash the wound and change the dressing every day for a week. Soon I was fully recovered and riding my bike again but with a lot more caution. I still have a small blue scar below my right knee, possibly still with some small bits of gravel in it, today!

When school started again in September, 1952, I was moved to what we called the "Top Class". It was actually for eight-to-eleven-year-olds; I was only six-and-a-half at the time and infants' school was supposed to be for five-to-seven-year-olds. Why I was moved so soon I have no idea. I certainly did not have the ability for it. The classroom was furnished with desks, which sat two children. Fortunately, I sat next to a clever girl who understood everything, whereas I struggled, so she helped me. Also, the teacher, Miss Longhurst, was kind to me and this helped me to relax and actually follow some of what was being taught.

Now I was in the "Top Class" I mixed with big boys up to eleven years old. I don't remember fights in the playground (as occurred in other schools that I attended later). However, when a dispute did happen there were usually several boys on either side of the argument and instead of fighting or even shouting at each other they would start to claim how many people they could collect to settle the difference of opinion by violence. For example, if a boy had several uncles he would say, "I have my father, older brother and four uncles to help me defeat you." Or, if their father was a farmer he might say, "I will bring my father and his workers."

In one such dispute I offered to the side with whom I wanted to gain favour my father, his nursery workers and my cousin Karl-Heinz and his friends from Germany. Just how I thought I would get my father and his workers to agree to this I had no idea. Moreover, how was I going to get Karl-Heinz and his friends to come all the way from Hamburg when I didn't speak German, never mind how was I going to pay for their journey? Even so, my offer seemed to be accepted by my side and as no one questioned the logistics of what I had suggested, the opposing side seemed at that point to accept defeat.

There were several characters in Warburton; one was a man called Alf. He was small man, whose face was wrinkled and weathered from working on the land for many years. He seemed very old to me and dressed in old working clothes and a small hat. He worked on the CWS farms in the area but sometimes came to work for my father. His speciality was that he looked after a Shire horse, which pulled various farm implements (from a plough to a cart). Every time I saw the horse it looked dirty, with its feet, coat and tail spattered with mud.

One day, I saw him and another man leading the horse along the lane by our neighbour's house across the road. He called to me and asked if I wanted to ride on the horse. Excitedly I crossed the road and the other man lifted me on to the horse. I had no idea that I would be so high up. We set off down the lane, with me desperately gripping the horse's mane for fear of falling off. After about a hundred yards they stopped the horse and lifted me off. I was very glad to get my feet on terra firma again.

As an example of how much he looked after the horse, a few weeks later on a Saturday the Lymn Mayday parade took place. This was a big event and we were taken to see it. There were bands, girls' dance and marching troops, and horse-drawn and tractor-drawn floats representing various elements of business, farming and the community. Suddenly came a number of Shire horses. Alf (who was dressed in his Sunday-best grey suit, a white shirt and tie) came first, leading his horse. Alf's calves were encased in highly polished, tight-fitting leather leggings and on his feet he had brightly-polished black boots. I could not at first believe it was Alf. He looked very smart and was smiling and waving to the crowd that lined the pavement on both sides of the road. Even more impressive was his horse. It looked immaculate with its coat shining and was beautifully groomed. The white hair around its hooves was perfectly clean and brushed so that it flowed in the wind. The hooves themselves were scrubbed white and the black leather bridle with which Alf was leading the horse was glistening in the sun. Above all it was bedecked in horse brasses from head to tail. The horse flicked its tail with pleasure as it proudly led the other horses. What a complete contrast from the rather dishevelled little man and mud-encrusted horse I was used to seeing.

The procession began at one end of the town and ended in a field at the other end. In the field was a funfair with coconut stalls, dodgem cars, two-seat swing-boats etc. There, Helen showed me how to sit in the swing-boat and alternately pull on my rope so that she and I made the swing move higher and higher. My favourite stall was the candyfloss stall; I just loved the spun sugar piled on to a stick, which when eaten melted into a sweet sticky mess in one's mouth.

Two other people I can remember clearly were brothers Hubert and Ken. Ken worked for my father; he was a keen and conscientious worker whose working attire consisted of blue overall trousers with a khaki ex-army shirt and blouse-type jacket. Whenever he met Helen and myself, he would tell us a joke.

I don't know what his brother Hubert did but he always wore a suit and tie. He drove a very small three-wheeler Bond mini-car, propelled by a small air-cooled motorbike engine mounted on the single-front-wheel assembly. It had a windscreen but no roof. When it rained one could put up a hood. There were only two seats and it was started by pulling a lever inside the car (there was no starter motor).

One day Hubert was driving his car along a country lane when he came across a large herd of cows coming the other way. Hubert stopped to let the cows pass by him. What he had not reckoned with was the fact that the cows had been feeding all day and were now evacuating their large intestines. By the time the cows had passed, and because his car was open and so low to the ground, he was covered in cow excrement and similarly the car was full of it.

In early 1953 my parents decided they wanted a dog, so we all went one Saturday to Manchester Dogs' Home and, after some searching, they saw this forlorn looking Fox Terrier. Maybe because Henry could remember Evy having such a dog he decided we should have it. It took a few days before we could collect it and in the meantime my mother thought of a name. As Queen Elizabeth was due to be crowned in June, and because the dog was female, it was decided to call her Queenie. She became a firm favourite and lived until the early 1960s.

Christine and Henry Frank on their wedding day
Devon 24.07.1940

Christine and Henry Frank. Paignton, Devon, UK early September
1941

Christine, Helen, Peter and Henry Frank
Golden Sands Holiday Camp,
Rhyl, North Wales, U.K. summer 1949

Helen and Peter Frank sitting on running board of our first car an Austin 16 saloon 1950

Christine, Peter, Henry and Helen Frank,
Waldtraut Hagel, behind Adolf Blaschke.
Lane End Farm Warburton, Cheshire, England 27.08.1950

Karl-Heinz, Helen, Hildegard, Peter and Brigitte in front of Austin 16
Tourer Hamburg summer 1951

Peter Lederhosen & Janka, Henry with Austrian hat, Helen in slacks
and my mother Austrian Dirndl, St.Gilgen1951

Chapter 8

The Plant Nursery, Marbury, Northwich, Cheshire

My father, having managed the CWS nursery for six years, started to think about his next career move. He wanted to become a horticultural advisor in what was then the Ministry of Agriculture and Fisheries (known as the "Ministry of Ag & Fish"). He saw this as an interesting, secure job with a good pension, where he could pass on his by now extensive experience and knowledge to other nurserymen. To do this, at that time, he needed to pass the highest examination in horticulture "The National Diploma of Horticulture".

As far as I can remember he took it twice, once in 1951 and then again in 1952. The first time he cut his finger while demonstrating how to take cuttings and therefore could no longer take part in the exam. The second time he failed on his digging because the examiner did not like the way he dug the ground. I have a feeling that in those days one could only take the exam three times so he was reluctant to take it again as it would prevent him from achieving his ultimate career goal.

He wanted to move on from being manager of the CWS nursery at Warburton, and began to consider his options (in other words, another managerial job or possibly striking out and running his own nursery business — but this was difficult because he did not have the capital to buy an ongoing business or to set one up from scratch).

The idea looked fairly hopeless until, some time in early 1953, he saw an advertisement in the local paper for a nursery to rent with land, cold frames and heated green houses. (Cold frames are enclosed structures about 18 inches high that can be covered by a frame of transparent material; they are used to protect plants from adverse weather, primarily excessive cold or wet.) One weekend soon after, we went to see the nursery. It was owned by a large British chemical company at a place called Marbury near Northwich in

Cheshire. It was ten miles from Warburton, so easily reachable by car in about thirty minutes. We had recently sold the Austin 16 Tourer and bought a blue Vauxhall 12 Tourer of a more recent vintage.

The main part of the nursery was a walled kitchen garden of about an acre in size, where flowers, fruit and vegetables had been produced for the family and staff of the nearby hall. Within it, there was a south-facing lean-to vinery built on a very low brick base. The vinery took nearly the total width of the inside north wall. In front of this were cold frames. In the middle of the inside of the west wall was a conservatory, which had a raised brick-built soil bed containing two large camellia shrubs: one produced white flowers, the other pink. On the back wall was a tall mimosa that reached to the roof.

The rest of the walled garden was divided into square plots, four in number separated by wide gravel paths edged with thick, upright, blue slate-like stones. The two northern and southern plots were also separated by beautifully manicured yew hedges on either side of the gravel paths.

To the west of the walled garden was some land and four free-standing (then modern) greenhouses, heated by a gravity circulation boiler. On the other side of the wall from the conservatory was a potting shed with a flagstone floor. To the south of the walled garden was another piece of land, again about an acre in size. Attached to the outside of the north wall was a row of low building. Some were for storage of fruit and vegetables and some were the living quarters for the garden staff in days gone by, known as "Bothies."

The nursery was immaculate, every tool in its correct place, the paths weeded and swept, the edging stones perfectly aligned, the fruit trees and yew hedges pruned, and all the glasshouses painted. I remarked to my father how tidy it was. He replied that the reason the current tenant was leaving was that he spent so much time on upkeep he could not make the place pay.

My parents decided they would like to have their own business but the problem was they did not have the capital necessary to buy stock plants, a suitable vehicle such as a delivery van or estate car, or a rotovator to till the land. So, my father wrote to his cousin Herbert in London and asked for a loan to cover the above items. Herbert agreed to lend the money so my parents decided to apply for the tenancy and were successful. The chemical company agreed that we could rent accommodation in one of their converted prisoner-of-war huts so we had somewhere to live. I describe the huts a little later. I was very excited at leaving Warburton, especially the school. I told everybody who would listen to me that we were moving a whole ten miles away.

My father's plan was to operate the same business model as he had employed in Warburton (cash crops such as bedding plants, flowers, potatoes, tomatoes, lettuce and fruit from the many fruit trees around the inside walls), but his main focus was to be on Alpines and herbaceous plants, for which he had gained a high reputation. He bought a Howard rotovator, stock plants, seeds and fertiliser, and a second-hand Ford V8 Shooting Brake, painted battleship grey. The vehicle had a wood-and-glass structure from the front passenger doors to the rear doors, enabling the transport of virtually anything — from us as a family to plants and even machinery such as the Rotovator. He finally sold the Vauxhall Tourer once we had moved.

A couple of days before we moved, my parents cleared out of the Lane End Farmhouse all the things they decided they did not want or could not take with them. I remember my father building a big bonfire and even the old pram he had bought when Helen was born was burned. The children from across the road came to watch the fire and the boy said the burning pram looked like a flaming chariot.

I think we moved on a Saturday and my father obtained permission from the CWS to use their farm lorry to move all our possessions and some stock he had bought from them. The truck was a big red Commer three-and-a-half-ton lorry. When all our personal possessions had been loaded onto it I was allowed to ride on the top of the load as far as the nursery, where the stock plants were loaded. My excitement was beyond description.

Once the stock plants had been loaded, I was then allowed to ride in the cab with the driver and somebody else who was helping with the move. Again, I was totally thrilled; all my dreams had come true. My father drove the also fully-loaded Ford V8 (from then on known purely as the "V8" or the van or sometimes the "Shooting Brake") and my mother drove the Vauxhall Tourer with Helen and Queenie the dog.

The gardens and hall were part of what was known variously as Marbury Park, Marbury Estate or Marbury Camp. The reason the whole complex had several names was because in times past a noble family had owned the whole area and built a French Chateau-style hall. The land around was planted with trees in the traditional parkland manner. The hall building faced a lake called Marbury Mere, which extended towards an old Cheshire village called Great Budworth, and at that end it was known as Budworth Mere.

The grounds around the hall were landscaped with pleasure gardens, lawns, yew hedges, wide paths and stone stairs reaching down to the mere and to other low-lying areas around the hall. It was also known as "the estate" because the family had owned considerable land in the surrounding countryside. At some time, the family had died out. Ultimately, in the 1920s it was sold and made into a country club, and judging by photographs taken at the time to advertise the club it was the height of elegance and luxury. The owners of the club even built an outdoor swimming pool in the grounds.

The phrase "Marbury Camp" came into being because, during the war, the army commandeered the hall and the estate. The land immediately to the east and west of the hall itself was converted into a prisoner-of-war camp. Wooden barrack huts and corrugated iron Nissan huts were erected. The most famous prisoner was a German soldier called Bert Trautmann, who stayed on after the war and became a footballer and long-term goalkeeper for Manchester City Football Club. The British Army guards and officers were stationed in the hall itself.

Towards the end of the war part of the Polish Free Army was billeted in the hall and, after the war, the chemical company bought the hall and surrounding land. The company was short of labour for its local factories and also short of housing for the married workers. Realising that if the part of the Polish Free Army stationed in the hall was returned to what was then a Poland under Russian domination, they would (at least) be imprisoned, and more likely shot as traitors. So, the chemical company offered them employment and the right to remain in the hall. It was turned into a Polish workers' hostel. A warden was employed and one of the Polish officers was appointed deputy-warden, as many of the Polish soldiers spoke very little or no English. Cooks from the Polish contingent were recruited so that the inmates could enjoy Polish meals.

I can only vaguely remember us arriving in Marbury. We drove to the long hut that my mother insisted we called a bungalow. Inside, it was divided with brick-built walls into a bathroom, toilet, large eat-in kitchen, living room and two bedrooms. My parents put what furniture would fit into the "bungalow". Then my father, with the helpers from the nursery in Warburton, took the V8 and Commer lorry to the nursery, where they unloaded the stock-plants. Later, our beds were put together and made and we slept the first night in our new home.

The rest of the furniture and other items, including the beautiful old bamboo bedroom furniture and two lovely old Windsor chairs, were stored in the "bothies" together with my parents' cabin trunks that had originally accompanied them from Poland and Austria. It was said that the items would be stored in the "bothies" on a temporary basis until the business had made enough money for us to build a nice house. This never happened and all the items slowly rotted away in the damp.

At the end of the war the chemical company had converted the huts into dwellings, installing electricity, water and sewage disposal, and dividing the huts with internal brick-built walls. The Nissan huts were replaced in situ with brick single-storey dwellings, which were more attractive. The east and west groups of converted huts became known as East Park and West Park.

My parents introduced themselves to the warden of the hall, who at the time was an Englishman with an RAF-type handlebar moustache. He and his wife and three daughters lived in a long bungalow situated in the Hall's courtyard. The deputy-warden, a former Polish officer, had a flat in the hall itself. He had a wife, three sons and a daughter. They all spoke Polish at home in the flat. I can remember the boys' bedroom. It was huge and centrally heated, with three beds around the walls and a large table in the centre of the room. Some years later we played endless games of Monopoly on that table during the weekends and holidays when it was too wet or cold to play outside.

Originally, I became friendly with the eldest boy and played with him until I met the youngest daughter of the English warden. She was lovely and I fell head-over-heels in love at the age of seven. I imagined how we would grow up together, marry and have a family. I can remember us sitting together and when the eldest boy of the Polish deputy-warden came to join us we both told him to go away, as we wanted be alone together.

It was 1953, Coronation year, and the English warden had a television in his bungalow. We, as a family, were invited to watch it. The inside of their bungalow was like a palace to me, with fitted carpets, a proper three-piece suite and matching curtains. Drinks were served out of cut-glass crystal.

Soon after Coronation day I went looking for the youngest daughter and could not find her. I knocked on the door of her bungalow but there was no answer. I went home thinking they must have gone out for the day. The next morning, I told my mother and she replied, "You will not see her again, they have gone away." I asked where they had gone and she explained that, two days before, the police had arrested the English warden for embezzling hostel funds. His wife and daughters had gone to live with her sister somewhere and I never saw the youngest daughter again — yet another of my many disappointments in life. The warden was found guilty and sentenced to three years in jail.

We initially lived in 184 East Park, not far from the swimming pool but at least five minutes' walk from the nursery, which (as winter approached) my father found onerous, as he had to stoke the coke-burning boiler every three-to-four hours, depending on how cold it was in the night. His winter ritual before he finally managed to afford a reliable, automatic oil heating system was as follows:

Before leaving the nursery around 5.00 p.m. he would stoke the boiler and then come home and sit in his chair by the fire and fall asleep until our mother had prepared the evening meal. Having eaten, he used to listen to the 6.00 p.m. BBC news, and then the weather forecast, on the radio. After having bought our first television set in 1954 he would watch these programmes on the only channel, which was the BBC.

Afterwards he might help us with our homework, do some paperwork, chat with us all or read the paper. Then he would fall asleep again until about 8.30 p.m., when he would wake up and at about 9.00 p.m., he went to stoke the boiler again. He came back after about twenty minutes and sat and read the paper or watched the television and then slept again in his chair.

Some time between midnight and 1.00 a.m. he would again stoke the boiler and when he returned again fell asleep in the chair until about 3.00 or 4.00 in the morning, when he would yet again have to stoke the boiler. On his return he would finally be able to crawl into bed and sleep until about 7.30 or 8.00 a.m. Fortunately he had a worker, who on his arrival at 8.00, would stoke the boiler, so my father could have breakfast before going to the nursery.

One night, while we still lived on East Park, he went to stoke the boiler and decided to adjust one of the valves in a greenhouse. While bending over to reach the valve he banged his head so hard on one of the pipes that he knocked himself out and lay for a few minutes until he came to. My mother, thinking this was very funny, told me about it when she came to wake me up in the morning. The story frightened me because all I could think about, even at my young age, was what would have happened if he had been killed or very badly injured, and how would my mother have managed? She did not have the experience, knowledge or skill to run the nursery. I simply don't know how we would have survived.

I can't remember much of those early days in Marbury except that my parents worked very hard to establish the nursery and hence the business. My sister and I were expected to help but, as I had never before worked and was just about to have my seventh birthday, I found this very difficult. This became a challenge for my parents because they (especially my mother) could not give me the attention I was used to receiving from them.

Easter was relatively early that year and afterwards Helen and I were sent to our new school. My parents decided to send us to Winnington School, which took both infant and primary school children. On the first day my mother took us in the V8 and deposited Helen in the primary part and me in the infant section. I remember our class teacher was a Miss Barker, a stern, old-style teacher who would not tolerate any nonsense.

The classroom was very close to one of the factories of the chemical company, the noise from which was incredible, with sirens and hooters going off all the time and the crash of coal being loaded into trucks to be taken to the furnaces. After the quiet, serene surroundings of Warburton School it was hell on earth for me, and I was petrified by the noise. The other children just accepted it. They not only heard it in the school but also, as most of them lived in the surrounding terraced houses, they were accustomed to it day and night.

The next day my mother told us we had to take the school bus that was provided to take children from our area directly to the school. She took us to the bus stop and gave each of us four old pence (the fare being two old pence each way). I must have relied on Helen to show me how to get on the bus and where to sit.

At the end of the school day, before the return journey, Miss Barker assembled all the children outside the infants' part of the school and marched us to the school gates. One child was given the privilege of carrying a red flag at the head of the procession. I can't remember what happened at the school gates: perhaps Helen was there and I got on the bus with her and she showed me where to get off, as there were at least two or three stops before ours.

We would go to the nursery and wait for my mother to finish her work. She would finish earlier than our father, as she had to take us home and prepare the evening meal. Helen would recount every detail of her day while, when my mother asked me the question "How was your day at school?", I would reply "All right." I replied the same thing during my whole time at school!

A few weeks later my mother lost her handbag, which had ten pounds in it. She stopped at a shop and when getting back into the shooting brake she put her handbag on top of the car, got in and drove off. In 1953 ten pounds was a lot of money — more than two weeks' wages for a working person. Also, she had lost her driving licence (which was also in the bag). Luckily a few days later a man came to the nursery with the bag, saying he had found it in the road. The relief to both my mother and father was immense.

As I have already said, it was Coronation year and as our class project to celebrate the event, Miss Barker decided we should plant red, white and blue bedding plants in the shape of "ER II" to commemorate the crowning of the new Queen Elizabeth. Miss Barker found a bare patch of earth, in which we put the plants and watered them and, lo-and-behold, they flowered in the planned shape in time for the Coronation.

My father's plan for the nursery was to continue as he had in Warburton, producing herbaceous and Alpine plants and selling them directly to shops and to the wholesale trade. So he, as I said above, bought a lot of stock from the CWS nursery in Warburton and planned to grow it on, so that the plants could be split and half of the split plants would be sold. Before leaving the nursery in Warburton he had informed his customers that he was setting up on his own and would be able to supply them with the same high quality plants he had provided from the nursery at Warburton.

Three things happened which prevented him from doing this. Firstly, as he contacted his previous customers many of them told him that actually they would not be buying from him because they did not want to break their existing loyalty to the CWS. Secondly, many of the shops were actually Co-operative shops that were duty-bound to buy from the CWS (although they had previously said they would buy from him). Thirdly, he discovered that the soil in Marbury had a very high pH value (which meant it was very alkaline) due to the chemical factory a couple of miles away, which mainly made caustic soda (an alkaline chemical compound). In those days there were no pollution controls and some of the chemical compound was blown out of the factory chimneys during the production process. Alpine plants and many herbaceous plants want acidic soil, or at least pH-neutral conditions, to thrive.

When he first visited Marbury he noticed that, outside the kitchen gardens, many large rhododendron shrubs were growing profusely. These shrubs normally only thrive in acidic or at least pH-neutral soil conditions, so he assumed that the same soil conditions would be suitable for Alpine and herbaceous plants — but this was not the case. So his business plan, as it would be called today, had to be urgently re-thought. He realised that he was going to run out of cash very quickly. He did two things. Firstly, as it was Coronation year, he grew (from seed) lots of red, white and blue bedding plants such as salvias, alyssum and lobelia. Secondly, he had Alf come from Warburton one Saturday and clear the large patch of land to the south of the walled garden. There he planted potatoes.

As the bedding plant seeds germinated, he had several of the women from Warburton nursery come over on a couple of weekends and prick out the germinated seeds into boxes. Once these had been hardened-off in cold frames he began to sell them, as many people wanted to show their patriotism and celebrate Queen Elizabeth's Coronation by having their gardens full of red, white and blue flowers.

At this time, he had very few, if any, sales outlets except for local shops and possibly the Manchester wholesale market, and of course direct sales from the nursery, but he managed to sell all he had grown and in fact grew more as the Coronation approached. On the day before the Coronation there was a last-minute rush to plant-up gardens. He sold most of his remaining stock that day and took one hundred and ten pounds in cash. Today that would be between three and four thousand pounds. As a result, he had sufficient cash to fund his family and business through the summer.

Then the potato crop was ready. He sold them to local greengrocers, other shops and even directly from the nursery. Before one entered the walled garden there was a large gate and open area and to the right was a small single-story hut with a flat roof. The walls were made from Fibro-board, which had a yellow coloured exterior. Many years later, when I went to Australia with my firm in the mid-1970s, I saw many houses built from this cladding material. This hut was called "the office" as it housed the telephone on a table, the poison cupboard (that, although there was a key in the lock of the cupboard door, I never saw locked), and one or two other items of furniture.

In the office my father opened his one and only fruit-and-vegetable shop. He found a pair of scales in the nursery and, together with the potatoes, cucumbers, tomatoes and fruit that he grew and the occasional box of oranges, onions and carrots that he bought from a local wholesaler, he began his own fruit-and-vegetable retail business.

There was one shop on the estate based on East Park. It was a general grocery store and, although it competed in some areas, the fruit and vegetables from the nursery were generally fresher. Our customers came mainly from East and West Park and some from surrounding villages, especially on a Sunday morning because in those days we were the only fruit and vegetable shop open on a Sunday morning.

In addition, Poles came from the Hall especially to buy fruit. The problem was that many of them spoke little or no English so my mother had to serve them, as she spoke Polish. Because my parents often worked in other parts of the nursery there was a hand-bell that customers could ring to summon one of my parents. Unfortunately, the bell was stolen, so the V8 was parked outside the office with the driver's side-window open and a note on the windscreen stating that for service one should press the horn. The above kept the business going financially but father realised it was not going to survive unless he could replace the growing and selling of herbaceous and Alpine plants that had proved infeasible.

He came up with idea of potted plants which he could grow in the greenhouses and sell to the wholesale markets. He reasoned that, as people were becoming more prosperous, they did not want to spend all their leisure time gardening. Instead they wanted simple, easy-to-maintain gardens with a lawn and shrubs, so that they had time to go out in their newly-acquired cars bought on hire-purchase. But they still wanted to have flowers and greenery in the house, so what better way than to supply this burgeoning market than with indoor pot plants.

He started with cyclamen, which he grew from seed, and then other smaller ornamental and novelty plants such as one that had green and silvery leaves (caused by it absorbing traces of aluminium from the soil) and another whose leaves would close together when stroked, plus both green and variegated ivies and maidenhair ferns. He began growing these plants in the second half of 1953 in the greenhouses of the nursery.

Unfortunately, he was limited to using only three of the four greenhouses that were, at that time, heated — because of an agreement with the chemical company that they had the use of one of them for the whole of 1953 to produce plants for its gardens, surrounding the factories and offices a couple of miles away. But at least it meant they shared some of the heating costs with him.

He managed to sell most of what he produced through the wholesale trade but it was not enough to properly finance the business and provide for his family. However, as Christmas approached there was more demand and he also began to make holly wreaths. Fortunately, as well as the rhododendrons, there was a row of holly trees nearby, with a lot of berries, from which to make the wreaths.

Then, from somewhere, he got an order for two hundred or more wreaths to be delivered within a few days. I remember my mother and father working through several nights to produce them. They even managed to teach me how to bind the moss on to the frame while they wired up sprigs of holly to be stuck into the moss. This order, plus the increased Christmas wholesale trade in plants, created enough money to keep the business going through the first few lean months of 1954. January, February and most of March were always quiet in terms of business because people had spent their savings over Christmas and the new year, so there was no demand for what were considered non-essential items such as plants.

By the end of February or early March he had just ten pounds in the bank so he went to his bank manager to ask for an overdraft (as he had a crop of Hydrangeas that would be ready for sale in April and May). Unfortunately, the bank manager refused him an overdraft, saying he did not believe the nursery was a viable business and because it was a rented property, he had no security to offer.

The manager did suggest he take a stall on Northwich market, to which my father said, "I am a grower with a certain reputation in the wholesale trade and it could hurt my reputation to be selling on a market stall." The manager replied, "Well, if that is the case you will have to go bankrupt!" This jolted my father and he then realised he had no other alternative but to try to sell on the market, and asked the manager if he knew how to get a stall on the market.

The manager gave him the name of the market superintendent. My father went to him and asked if he could have a stall. The superintendent told him there was a stall available but he would have to get the agreement of the town councillor, who was responsible for the market. At the time Northwich market was open on a Friday and Saturday and the biggest and most important nursery business in the area had a permanent stall, which they only opened on a Friday. So when my father went to see the councillor he said my father could have a stall but only on a Saturday as he did not want to upset the owners of the big nursery, who were longstanding stall holders on the market, particularly as the only available stall was very close to their stall.

Chapter 9

Northwich Market

The following Saturday I was rudely awakened early from my bed and told I had to go with my father to the market. My mother would look after the nursery and take care of any customers that came, and my sister was told to stay at home and look after the house. The night before, my father had assembled various boxes of house plants, herbaceous and Alpine plants (that had survived but that he had not been able to cultivate), tin vases of cut daffodils (which he had grown in the heated greenhouses) and boxes of flowering bulbs. We loaded all of them into the V8 and set off for the market.

It was the first time I had been there and I remember we managed to park outside the big, heavy wooden double-doors, which led into the market hall. Before the doors were steep, uneven steps that one had to climb. I had to take the boxes of plants out of the van and carry them up the steep steps and through the heavy doors. Fortunately, the stall was nearby. As I gave the boxes to my father, he took out the pot plants and arranged them on the stall, which was shelved so he could display them as well as possible. The herbaceous and Alpines he put on the floor under the stall, still in their boxes. The bulbs also remained in their respective boxes but were put on the stall.

He had bought some blank yellow cards, about the size of a playing card, on which he wrote the price of each pot, herbaceous and Alpine plant. He did the same for the bunched daffodils and priced the bulbs by the dozen. He had also brought newspaper in which to wrap the plants and cut flowers, and had bought brown paper bags for the bulbs; lastly, he had an oblong, open tin box, which he used as a cash register or till.

I stood watching as the first people walked by. Suddenly someone stopped and asked my father about a particular potted plant. My father answered his or her question and they said they would like to buy it. The plant was wrapped in newspaper and the money handed over and we had made our first sale. Trade was fairly brisk for the first hour, from approximately 8.30 a.m. to 9.30 a.m.. Then it began to slow. The early morning shoppers consisted mainly of shop assistants who began work at 9.00 a.m. and women doing their early morning shopping before going home to cook the lunch.

After 9.30 a.m. fewer people were passing by the stall, and in fact the whole market hall became quiet. Then a well-dressed couple stopped and began talking to my father and suddenly he took a brown paper bag from the pile and began drawing on it. I could not understand what he was doing. He continued in conversation with them for some time, during which other people were stopping and looking at the plants but then, seeing my father in intense conversation, walked away. After about half an hour my father gave the couple the paper bag with his drawings. They thanked him, took the paper bag with them and walked away.

I was angry with my father because I knew we had not got much money and market sales were important. I told him that while he was chatting to the couple several people had stopped to look at the plants but he had ignored them, so missing possible sales. He did not seem too worried about this but said to me, "Why don't you try selling to them?" I replied, "I am not yet eight and I don't know what to say." He replied, "It is easy. If they stop and start looking at a plant, ask them if you can help them. If they ask the price of a particular plant, read the price on the yellow label and ask if they want to buy it. If they say "yes", take it down from the stall, wrap it in newspaper and hold out your hand for the money." I was shocked that my father thought I would be able to accomplish a sale at my tender age.

Soon, someone came by and began talking to my father and while he was deep in conversation an old lady carrying two bags of shopping walked by the stall and stopped and began to look at a plant, an ivy plant if my memory serves me correctly.

She looked round, saw my father was deep in conversation and was just about to walk on when I, with great trepidation, asked her, "Can I help you madam?" She looked me up and down as if to say, "What are you to do with this stall?" But she actually said, "How much is that little ivy plant?" I read out the label, which stated the price was one shilling and three pence, and went on to say, "Would you like it? — if so, I can wrap it for you." She said she wanted the plant. I took the plant from the stall and wrapped it as she was getting her purse out of one of her bags. On opening her purse, she gave me an old shilling piece and three-penny bit and I gave her the plant, which she put into one of her bags. I thanked her and put the money in the "cash register" and she turned and walked away. I had made my first sale and my father was still talking to the same person, who in the end did not buy anything.

That was the first Saturday of many on Northwich Market. Much later my father told me he had taken ten pounds that day, and realised that if he could do this every Saturday that would be enough to help the business and his family through the lean periods when he did not have a crop to sell wholesale.

He then got permission to have a stall on the Friday, which my mother managed. Then she began to sell at Frodsham Market, another Cheshire town, on a Thursday, from where she always brought back the most wonderful fish and chips for our evening meal. She also sold on Runcorn Market, again in Cheshire, on a Tuesday, for a short while.

The old market hall at Northwich was demolished in the late 1960s, when much of Northwich was rebuilt. In all, my parents had a stall on Northwich Market for over twenty years, through to 1975 when they finally gave up their market stall in the newly built market building (which was by no means as interesting as the previous one).

On the second Saturday, my father left me on the stall on my own during a quiet period while he went to buy something. When he had gone a man came up and asked about some of the herbaceous plants under the stall. To me they looked like clumps of muddy earth with a few straggly roots and one or two leaves or stalks. I could not imagine why anyone would want to buy such disgusting dirty things, and as none had been sold during our first Saturday, I thought they were more or less worthless.

Different plants were in different boxes, all labelled as to what they were, and there was a price on each box. The man read the labels and then asked me how many he would get for the price shown, which varied from one shilling and six pence to two shillings and six pence, depending on the type of plant. Thinking they were worthless lumps of mud that we had not been able to sell the previous Saturday, and that my father would be delighted with me if I got rid of the lot in one go, I said the price was for a dozen so he said he would take a dozen of each sort. So, I took some newspaper and began to count them out and suddenly realised that none of the boxes contained a dozen of any of them. I was perplexed as to what to do because I had not learnt sufficient mental arithmetic to work out that if a dozen of the plants cost two shillings and six pence, then what would eight plants cost?

As I tried to explain this to the man, my father returned and indignantly I told him I was trying to sell all his lumps of mud and straggly roots and dead stalks at once, but that he had not brought a dozen of any of them. My father laughed and explained that the price was per plant. I was shocked: how could he sell such disgusting things, that had made my hands very dirty putting them on to the newspaper, and why would anyone want to spend so much money on one such plant?

My father explained to the man that the price was per plant and he replied, "Well I thought I was getting a real bargain until you arrived!" But the man understood and with good grace bought one of each of the herbaceous plants, which came to ten shillings — a princely sum then, now fifty pence. I asked my father how he could have the cheek to sell such things for so much money. He explained that the separate plants would produce beautiful flowers within a year. Each plant would grow and spread so that they could be split and one half could be planted elsewhere, and that the plants would live many more years. This was my introduction to herbaceous plants.

Later that day the well-dressed couple returned with the paper bag in hand and again engaged my father in a long conversation. Every so often he would add or amend some scribbles, as they appeared to me, to the paper bag and again after about half an hour the couple left, paper bag in hand. While my father was deep in conversation with the couple, I had to deal with the passing trade, selling an ivy plant here or a maidenhair fern there, because I knew we had to sell our plants to survive — not just talk to people and scribble on a paper bag.

Again, on the third Saturday the couple returned with the paper bag and again my father spent half an hour or more in conversation with them — modifying yet again the scribbles on the paper bag. Then, as always, the couple walked away with the paper bag, not having bought anything.

On the fourth Saturday they returned with the paper bag. This time I was determined to see what was going on because it was time to tell my father he could not expect an eight-year-old to do all the business while he passed the time of day scribbling on a paper bag and chatting to people who didn't buy anything. But something was different: they were talking to my father and he was writing out a list with prices alongside. He then added up the list and turned to the couple and said, "That will be five pounds one shilling and six pence, but we can forget the one shilling and six pence." From his wallet the man took a large white piece of paper that had black printed letters and numbers on it and gave it to my father.

I had heard of five-pound notes but never seen one before. My father had just sold five pounds worth of stock in one go; I could not believe it. He then put all the plants he had just sold into three boxes and said that I would help carry them to the couple's car. They carried one box each and I carried the third. We loaded the boxes into the boot of the car and they drove away. I never saw the couple again. That evening my father showed us all the five-pound note. I had heard that workers in the chemical factory took home four pounds a week. My father, having dug these muddy clumps of earth from the ground, had sold them over a period of four weeks in half-hour sessions and had earned a quarter more than a chemical factory worker did for working a whole week.

Many years later, as I was coming to the end of my career in computer sales, I developed a sales course. One of the features of the course was to distinguish between product-selling and account- or client-management. As a way of keeping the course participants interested, I would relate the above story — how I was essentially performing the product sales role and my father the account- or client-manager role. I would quite openly admit that at eight years old my product knowledge of the plants I sold was very limited, and that a proper product salesperson would have extensive knowledge of his or her products. The main difference between a product salesperson and an account- or client-manager was that the latter not only had the extensive product knowledge necessary but also totally understood the customers' requirements, and could advise accordingly.

The market had a life of its own. There was an ebb and flow of people throughout the day. First the stallholders would arrive around 8 a.m. and bring their stock in from their vehicles. Some had fixed stalls, especially around the inner walls, which they could lock-up and hence only had to bring in replenishment stock. Others, like us, had to bring all our stock into the market and then take it home at the end of the day.

Then the early shoppers would begin to arrive from about 8.30 a.m. onwards and trade would often be very brisk for an hour or so. There was then a lull until about 10.30 a.m. when people from outside the town would begin to arrive, having come in by bus. About 12.00 midday it began to get quiet as customers went home for lunch. Business would pick up slowly from 2.00 p.m. onwards, becoming more busy as the afternoon wore on and ending with a rush as people finished work and as football spectators (it was always a 3.00 p.m. Saturday kick-off in those days) came out of the match (around 5.00 p.m.) and did their last-minute shopping.

Then about 5.45 p.m. it began to become quiet and it was time to pack up and either take unsold stock home or lock up the more shop-like stalls. At the same time, the market superintendent began to brush up the rubbish. This is what I mean when I talk about the ebb and flow of the market.

The original market hall that I first visited in 1954 was probably built in the 19th century. It had a cast iron structure, brick and timber walls and a part-slate, part-glass roof to allow light inside. It was two storeys in height but there was only the ground floor and a balcony round the whole hall at first floor level. Prior to us being there, stalls had been set up on the balcony but parts of the wood flooring and surrounding rail had become rotten so most of it was closed off for safety reasons.

The floor of the hall was buckled and very uneven. This was because of the subsidence that occurred in Northwich, caused by the extraction of salt (by pumping high-pressure water into the salt layer underground and then pumping out the resulting brine). No one knew where the water dissolved the salt, hence there was continuous subsidence in the area, resulting in some cases with old houses sinking overnight down to the first-floor windows. So, most buildings were built around a wooden or metal frame on a raft of wood or concrete so that as the building sank it could be jacked-up again to a safe height.

This was particularly true of the banks, which in those days contained heavy strong-rooms and safes. I remember the first time I was sent to get change for my fathers "cash till". He sent me with a pound note, telling me how many half crowns, two-shilling pieces, shillings, sixpences, three-penny bits, pennies and half-pennies I should get in exchange for the pound. I climbed three steps to enter the bank. By the early 1960s I was walking into the bank and the steps had disappeared. In the mid-1960s the bank was closed for a while and it transferred its business to a nearby empty shop, while the original building was jacked up to its previous height.

The market had many attractions for me; so many different interesting stalls selling cloth, shoes and bags from Manchester, knitting wool and yarn from Chester, a tool stall for tradesmen and handymen, a large butchers stall and a separate one selling cooked meat, a cheese stall that sold all the British varieties (if it sold any European ones it was probably the ball-like Dutch Gouda in its red wax covering). There was a book and magazine stall backing on to our stand, which first introduced me to Superman and Marvel-Man comics, and later to the pictures of nude women in magazines such as "Health and Efficiency", and finally the toy stall, which my father had to drag me away from to help him sell.

A year or two later a man came every Saturday all the way from near the Welsh border, where he had a record shop. He brought a selection of his records, particularly top-twenty hits, which he would play on a record player. This drew many young people to his stall, many of them my friends who would always come and say hello to me while we listened together to the latest hit songs. About the same time as the record stall arrived, a Polish lady set up a food stall to serve the local Polish community. It was opposite our Saturday stall and my father would buy smoked sausage from it and eat it out of the paper in which it had been wrapped.

There was also a small café in one corner of the market where I could have a three-course meal and a cup of tea or coffee for about two shillings. I loved the sights, sounds, smells and energy of the market and used to look forward to my Saturdays helping my father on the stall. There was also an outside market, and one of the stalls sold fruit from all parts of the world. The owner came from Liverpool and had many fruit shops there. It was said that he had so much demand that when a ship carrying fruit came into port, he always bought half the cargo.

One last stallholder I must mention had his stall on some waste ground that was used to park stallholders' vehicles once they had unloaded their wares at the big double-doors. He sold all sorts of household items, including ladies' handbags, kitchenware, cutlery, tea and dinner sets. His stock was loaded in a big furniture van and, depending on what he was selling at any point in time, he would display a quantity of those goods on the stall in front of the back of his van. He always sold in front of the stall so there was no barrier between him and his potential customers.

His sales technique was a bit like a Dutch auction. He would wait until a crowd had gathered, which it always did because the people knew they could get what they thought was a bargain from him. He would start with, say, a dinner service, which he somehow managed to hold in one hand. This included, say, six soup, dinner and dessert plates, plus a meat plate and even a couple of vegetable bowls. He would say, "Now ladies and gentlemen, I am selling this complete dinner service for not five pounds as you pay in some fancy shop, not even three pounds but two pounds seventeen shillings and six pence." None of the crowd would show any interest because they knew there was more to come.

Then, as though realising no one was interested he would say, "All right, I can see you are expecting more." He would then take a tea service, in the same pattern as the dinner service, from the various piles of crockery and somehow balance it on the outstretched arm that already held the dinner service and say, "You can have both the dinner and tea service", which included six side-plates, cups, saucers, a milk jug, sugar bowl and tea pot, "not for two pounds seventeen and six pence, not even two pounds and ten shillings, not even two pounds seven shillings and six pence but two pounds five shillings."

By this time the crowd really believed there was a bargain on offer and would stampede forward, waving their money at him, at which time he and his two assistants would very quickly and repeatedly assemble a dinner and tea service and put it into a customer's open shopping bag while collecting the money.

This performance would continue all day long, depending on the ebb and flow of the crowd, what goods he had to sell and what time of the year it was. Periodically he would return to the same products but offers and prices would vary depending on how much he thought he could get at any particular time of day.

Sometime in early 1955 I met a boy a few years older than me. His parents had a very successful fruit and vegetable stall on the outside market. They came from Droylsden on the east side of Manchester, where they had a very large market garden. When we were not busy, we would play on the waste ground or watch the man doing the quasi-Dutch auction.

Soon after we met, he asked me what football team I supported. Because my parents came from central and eastern Europe football was rarely, if ever, discussed so although I had heard friends talking about various teams, I had no idea about them at all, except I knew that in Northwich at that time there were two teams — Northwich Victoria and Witton Albion. I knew Northwich Victoria (or "Vics" as they are known) played on a ground behind the bus station, and Witton Albion had its ground behind the Plaza cinema. The boy said to me, "As you don't support any team at the moment, you can support my team — Manchester City — and to make sure you do not confuse them with Manchester United, City play in blue at home and United in Red."

I was so proud that I finally had a team to support — I could tell all my friends at school I was now a Manchester City supporter. The fact that I hadn't a clue about where the team's home ground was or the name of the manager or any of the team members, past or present, did not deter me at all; I was now, in my eyes, a fully-fledged Manchester City supporter. I have remained a supporter to the present day. However, I have to admit I am a closet supporter because I have hardly ever watched them play either at a football ground or on television, because if I do, they are bound to lose.

As we lived five minutes' walk from the nursery on East Park this added ten minutes to my father's nightly winter boiler-stoking routine. So, he asked if a bungalow was available on the West Park, which was considerably closer to the nursery. One became available in 1955 and we moved into number 5 West Park.

This had the advantage of being less than one minute from the nursery but the disadvantage of being half the size of the previous one. The kitchen and bathroom were tiny. Whereas before we could eat in the kitchen and the toilet was separate from the bathroom, now we had to eat in the living room and if someone decided to have a long bath and someone else had a desperate need for the toilet, the situation could get rather fractious. The living room and two bedrooms were half the size of the previous bungalow on East Park. How we managed I don't know but somehow it never bothered me — maybe because my mother always made it feel like our home. However, as time went on it took its toll on her.

Moving from East Park to West Park meant we had new neighbours; one of them was a woman who worked at the Hall as a cleaner. Her husband for some reason or other was on permanent disability benefit so there was not much money coming into the home. She supplemented her income by providing sexual services, particularly to the lonely Poles who lived in the Hall.

One day, as she was cleaning in the hall, a man who was not working asked her for sex. She agreed and it was decided that as they could not use his bed in the dormitory (because other people were sleeping there) they would go into the loft above. As they lay down on the floor of the loft it gave way. Fortunately, they both fell through on to an empty bed below. The noise woke the men who were sleeping and both of them were injured and could not work for a couple of weeks.

A further example of the poverty that surrounded us was a family of five who were very poor because the husband kept most of his wages for himself, thinking his wife could manage on thirty shillings a week (one pound and fifty pence in today's decimal currency), while he spent the rest on drink, cigarettes and betting on the horses. His wife was meant to feed and clothe the three children and herself, and pay for coal, electricity, rent and rates, all out of the money he gave her.

One day at about 4.30 p.m. I was in the general grocery shop on East Park that I mentioned earlier, and very quickly became aware of a terrible smell. The eldest girl of the family was holding a saucer on which was a fried egg, where instead of the yolk being yellow it was green. I quickly realised the smell was emanating from the egg, particularly the green yolk.

The girl was next in the queue to the person being served. The smell was so bad the person being served quickly finished buying what was needed and left. The girl advanced to the counter, where the owner said, "Why have you brought this smelly egg into my shop?" The girl explained that her mother had bought the egg, one egg, earlier in the day as this was to be the evening meal for the mother and three children, and when her mother had broken the egg, allowing it to drop into the hot frying pan, she realised she had been sold a rotten egg.

Having two other younger children to look after she sent the eldest to the shop with the egg to ask for a replacement or the money back. The owner said "I can't help it if I sold you a rotten egg; I am not going to replace it and I am not giving you your money back. Take that smelly egg out of my shop immediately." The girl left, clutching the saucer, and the mother and children went to bed hungry that night.

One consolation my father had when having to regularly stoke the boiler on cold winter nights was that Queenie, the dog, always accompanied him. The dog was his constant companion, day and night, except when, because she was a female dog, she was "on heat." Then she had to be kept indoors and was only let out on the lead, with the person taking her out having to carry a big stick to ward off the pack of male dogs that wanted to take advantage of her. When Queenie was "in season" all the dogs that could get out of their homes did so and surrounded either the van (in which she was put during the day) or our home at night.

I remember some very cold winters but no matter how cold it was the dogs would surround the house the whole night. The one thing for the owners was that if they could not find their dog, they would certainly find it either at the nursery around the V8 or around our home at night. Queenie did not mind being shut in the van. In fact she loved it. She loved being taken for a ride in it. She would stand on the front seat with her front paws on the dashboard and bark for the whole journey without stopping. Naturally she was only taken on journeys that were really necessary.

She loved having visitors, both at the nursery and at home, but when they came to leave if she was not held back, she would immediately attack them, ferociously. When people called at the nursery the tactic to prevent the person leaving having been savaged was to say, "Vansi" to Queenie, upon which she thought she was being taken for a ride. She would run to the van and willingly jump in. The door was then closed and she would happily remain in the van until she was let out. At home, a different tactic had to be employed, depending on whether the visitor was leaving via the back door or the front door. If by the back door, she had to be enticed (or more often dragged) out of the living room and put into the tiny hall, where the front door was. If the visitor was leaving via the front door she was put into the kitchen.

One morning my father had lingered over his breakfast a little too long and suddenly realised that he had to get to work, but had let his cup of tea go cold; on seeing the dog's water bowl was empty he poured the cold tea into it. The dog took one sniff and lapped it up, much to my father's surprise. From that day on, Queenie would not leave the house without having had her dish of tea. If for some reason she annoyed my father he would not put the sugar in the tea. She would begin to drink the tea and then, realising it was not sweet, would cock her head to one side and look at my father with disdain and continue to drink the tea. A similar thing happened if he served her tea without milk.

On Sundays my mother always cooked a wonderful roast and what remained was given to Queenie, who gulped it down. Every Sunday at about 1.00 p.m. the ice cream van came round and Helen or I was sent out to buy four wafers of ice cream for our dessert. Somehow, one Sunday Queenie got a lick of some left-over ice cream and she went wild, licking her food bowl and chasing it round the floor as she tried to ensure she had not missed the slightest morsel. So from then on, whenever she heard the ice cream man's bell (or later chimes) her head cocked to one side and she wagged her tail furiously, so much so that we began buying five wafers so Queenie could enjoy a whole one for herself.

Being a wirehaired fox terrier, her hair grew and became thick and matted. The first summer in Marbury was a warm one and Queenie began to pant a lot and was obviously suffering from the heat. Dog parlours were not common in those days but eventually my parents found one and

Queenie was taken to it and clipped. I was still in school and when I got home, I thought we had a different dog. She looked much thinner and her hair was very short and soft, and she smelled very nice. She obviously liked feeling cool in the summer and having a weight of matted hair removed from her. So, it became an annual ritual for Queenie that in late spring every year she was clipped and washed.

A further story about Queenie involved my mother's passion to have the fish carp served as the main course of the meal on the evening of Christmas Eve. This custom is still prevalent in parts of Central and Eastern Europe, particularly to my knowledge in Germany and Poland, from where my mother originated. My father hated carp but nevertheless for several years in the late 1950s and early 1960s my mother would serve carp on Christmas Eve. When presented with the dish my father, so as not too displease his wife, would manfully eat a few mouthfuls of the fish and then lose his temper, putting his plate on the floor to show his displeasure.

Although this only happened once a year, Queenie quickly realised that once the Christmas tree was put up in the house there was a special treat in store for her. Once she smelled the carp on the table she would sit by my father, gazing up at him and wagging her tail furiously. As soon as my father's plate reached the floor, she would immediately devour its contents. My father would berate my mother, saying, "How many times have I told you I don't like carp and especially don't want to eat it on the evening of Christmas Eve." My mother would shrug her shoulders and continue to sit and enjoy her carp.

Having finished her main course, she would then pacify my father by serving canned fruit, which he loved, or chocolate mousse with whipped cream — and once a Hungarian Doboschtorte, which took her a week to make from scratch.

The three- or four-times carp was served on Christmas Eve came to an abrupt end when, in 1962, on serving the carp we all notice it had a greenish tinge. My father immediately declared it was not fit for human consumption; my mother tried to eat it but very reluctantly had to agree with her husband that it was inedible. The crowning insult for my mother was when all the carp was scraped into the dog's bowl but even Queenie would not eat it. My father then declared that, once and for all, no more carp was to be served at home at any time ever again. However, this did not stop my mother serving other freshwater fish, as we shall see later.

As I mentioned in an earlier chapter, my mother always wanted to know what the future held. When she heard that there was a woman in the area who had a reputation for giving accurate readings, she made an appointment to see her. My father was furious: he did not believe in it and said she was wasting her time and his money.

The appointed day came and she took Helen with her. I stayed at home with my father, who continued to grumble about my mother. When she returned, he listened very attentively to what she had been told but continued to say the whole thing was a load of rubbish. I can only remember two things. Firstly, my mother said I would do well and would work with something that had not yet been invented. By that time the first commercial computers were still being developed but not many people knew what they were or did. I was nine at the time. Eleven years later I started as a computer operator and went on to join a UK computer firm, where I stayed for over thirty years, retiring as a sales director.

The second thing I remember is my mother saying that the lady was receiving the information she was giving them from the spirit world. My father immediately laughed and ridiculed them, until he was told that the spirit that the woman was in touch with was an old lady with grey hair, who wore a grey twin-set and had a necklace of black shells around her neck.

At that point my father became quiet and his complexion became very pale. He said the woman had described his mother Ilona Frank, who in later life had grey hair and wore a grey twin-set with a necklace of black coral! I met the same woman who had given my mother the reading twice or three times in my twenties, and she gave me readings which turned out be very accurate.

In October 1955 I had to be admitted into the Agnes Hunt and Robert Jones orthopaedic hospital in Oswestry. For some time, whenever I walked more than a short distance my legs became weak and after several visits to our doctor and specialists I was diagnosed as having knock-knees. The doctors said the cause was my large size and weight for my age. My thighs extended downwards to my knees in a "V" shape and then my lower legs spread out from my knees in an inverted "V". I could not put my ankles together — there was about a nine-inch gap between them.

I underwent an operation where they cut open the flesh on the inside of each knee and bolted a piece of flat metal to my thigh bones and my lower leg bones, so that as I grew the bolted metal plates would straighten my legs. I was in hospital for eight weeks and had to learn to walk again. My parents came every Sunday to see me. It was a round trip of around a hundred miles. Given how hard my parents worked, I now realise that what was then a two-hour drive both ways was a tremendous sacrifice out of their one partially-free day. They always brought me a present to cheer me up. This usually consisted of a Dinky Toy and I still have three of them.

The hospital was built as separate wards, all on the ground floor and connected by a central corridor. One side of each ward could be completely opened using folding doors. When open, our beds were wheeled out of the ward on to a terrace, as it was believed that fresh air (no matter how cold or hot) would expedite recovery. The only time we were not put outside was when it was raining or when a patient was very ill.

While there, every Saturday afternoon there was a film show on the ward. The one film I remember was the Glen Miller Story. The film and music enthralled me. Up until then I had always been frightened of films unless they were a comedy, and even they could sometimes make me anxious.

I came out of hospital just before Christmas 1955 and my parents sent me straight back to school, as they were worried that I had missed so much. I was still quite weak and could not walk very far, and suffered from pains in my legs as they became accustomed the steel plates and to bearing my weight again. I tried to help my father on the market but found I could not stand for long periods, and as there was nowhere to sit down, I found it very painful and tiring. My parents suggested I stay at home until late morning and then take the bus into town at lunchtime so my father could have a break and some lunch.

About the same time, the boy from the fruit and vegetable stall suggested we went to the matinee at the cinema, which started at 2.00 p.m. and ended a little after 4.00 p.m. This was a good solution because it allowed me to sit for a couple of hours, and so began my love of the medium of film.

Every Saturday I would get to the market around 12.00 p.m. and watch the stall while my father took a break, after which he would give me my pocket and lunch money. After lunch at the market café my friend and I would go to the "Regal" cinema and watch whatever was on. After the cinema we would go back to the market to help on our stalls until it was time to pack up and go home. This Saturday routine lasted for several years until my friend, who was about four years older than me, left school and began to work for his parents. Then he was expected to stay on the stall all day and our trips to the cinema came to an end.

On the morning of pancake Tuesday (Shrove Tuesday) in 1956 my teacher at Winnington Park primary school decided to encourage the pupils in her class to say how they would be celebrating pancake day at home that evening. Most, if not all, the contributions from the class came in the form of either whether the pancakes would be tossed or turned over using a spatula, or what kind of topping would be put on the pancake (Golden syrup being the most popular, followed by various flavours of jams and marmalades). I am sure my mother had made pancakes for us previously but I, being the only child in the class of foreign parents, had never heard of pancake Tuesday or the various toppings. I was devastated at not being able to make a contribution to the class discussion.

On reaching home that evening I begged my mother to make me a pancake so that, the next day, I could say that I too had had a pancake for my evening meal. My mother, who was very tired from working all day at the nursery, had already bought some ready-made meals so she would not have to cook. Given how tired she was, she was not exactly enthusiastic about making a pancake for me but I persisted and she finally relented.

Having made the pancake, I then said to her that golden syrup was my preferred topping. She told me we did not have any and I, being very fussy, did not eat jams or marmalade at that time. But she did have a lemon, which she cut in half and squeezed over the pancake. I was just about to protest when she liberally sprinkled sugar over the lemon juice and pancake, saying that is how she had eaten pancakes in Poland. I took a bite of the pancake, lemon juice and sugar, and it was delicious. I went to school the next day being able to tell everybody I had had a pancake the previous evening. I did not say that I had lemon juice and sugar on it as my classmates would not have understood. Since then my favourite pancake is with lemon juice and sugar.

By the mid-to-late 1960s my father was growing and selling eight-thousand cyclamen, six-thousand hydrangeas and later four-thousand azaleas per year. However, yet again there was a problem caused by the chemical company. As I have mentioned before, some of the alkaline product was carried up the tall factory chimneys and deposited on the surrounding countryside, including the nursery's glasshouses. This deposit darkened the glass and reduced the light, so making growing conditions more difficult. Henry complained to the chemical company, who would not admit liability but agreed to sell him gallon bottles of hydrochloric acid at a reduced price to wash the alkaline deposit from the glass. Although he diluted the acid it was still a very dangerous process because even the diluted acid, if accidentally splashed on skin or clothing (or worse still, splashed in the eyes) could cause significant injuries, plus there was the risk of falling through the glass. The greenhouses had to be washed once a year just before winter.

The other problem was that the greenhouses had to be heated from autumn until spring. Initially, when Henry took over the nursery, the heating system comprised a very inefficient coke-burning furnace, with no pump to assist the hot-water circulation. In order to maintain the heat required, he bought (again cheaply from the chemical company) rolls of clear polyethylene. He stuck the polyethylene on to the inside of the wooden frames that supported the exterior glass, so creating a type of double-glazing effect, which increased the temperature inside the glass houses by about 5 degrees.

Having improved the light conditions and increased the heat, he was successfully able to produce large volumes of pot plants for both wholesale and retail. He further improved the heating a year or so later by fitting a circulation pump for the hot water pipes and a fan to the furnace, which meant the coke was burnt more efficiently — producing more heat at a lower cost.

On top of all the above, a further cash revenue stream was quickly developed by providing the flowers, bouquets and buttonholes for weddings, and wreaths and crosses for funerals. Where my parents acquired the skill to do this I don't know, but they became well-known and built up quite a local reputation. I can remember people coming to the house in the evenings, and excited soon-to-be-married couples discussing the colour and quantity of what they wanted. On the other hand, we had to appear solemn when bereaved relatives came to discuss their requirements for a funeral. My father, who had beautiful handwriting, would write the required messages of condolence on white cards edged in black and would then attach them with wire to the wreath or cross.

When one of the Polish community died, the requirement was not just for very elaborate wreaths and crosses but also for black silk ribbons stamped with the name of the bereaved in gold block. For this my parents always had a long roll of inch-wide black silk ribbon and fortunately there was, at that time in Northwich, a small print works that could do the gold blocking. My parents and the printworks had to be very careful to have the correct spelling of the bereaved Polish person and any message of condolence (that would also be in Polish). I remember seeing the finished article and trying, without success, to read the name and message on the silk ribbon. Today it reminds me of that joke about the Pole who visits an English optician and when asked to read the letters on the card says, "Of course I can read the letters — I know him."

Chapter 10

Germany, Genevieve, Geneva and the Second Great Adventure

It was in the mid-to-late 1950s that I began to become aware of my parents' characteristics, habits, accents and friends. My father was the excitable, impatient Austrian and my mother the placid, stoic Pole. Both were heavy smokers: my mother smoked forty cigarettes a day and my father a pipe, the smoke of which he inhaled. He smoked Three Nun tobacco and a four-ounce tin lasted him about three days.

Before the Ronson Varaflame Gas lighter was invented my father used a box of matches a day. In the evening, as he sat reading the paper or watching the television, he littered the open-fire hearth with matches that he had failed to throw into the fire. My mother would become very angry but only the changeover to the gas lighter stopped the hearth and surrounding area from being strewn with spent matches.

I was only aware of them having foreign accents when speaking English much later in life, when I had acquired a video camera and heard them speak when replaying the video. However, when I was young, I was playing with some friends and all of a sudden one of them said to me in a Cheshire accent, "Don't your mum and dad speak funny." I told my parents about this and they admitted they spoke with Central and Eastern European accents but claimed, probably quite rightly, that their command of English was equal to or greater than most of our English neighbours.

As for friends, they had many, both British and mainland European ones (who had come to England as refugees after the war from Czechoslovakia, Germany, Poland etc). Because my parents were so welcoming and ever-eager to make friends, whatever a person's nationality, I was influenced by this — together with the various ideas and cultures that they brought into our home — which has allowed me to accept people for who they are.

As already mentioned, my mother was an inveterate smuggler. In 1955 she decided to visit her sister Waldtraut in Hamburg. Waldtraut's husband Jupp was the purchasing director of a cigarette firm and as such received many gifts and a very generous monthly allowance of cigarettes. Whist there, Jupp kept giving her unwanted gifts and cigarettes, to the extent that she accumulated (amongst other things) about three thousand cigarettes, at least two bottles of spirits, two of wine and a Montblanc fountain pen and propelling pencil. There was far too much to pack into the single suitcase she had arrived with so she went out and bought another one to transport all her booty home.

She was way above the duty-free limit but this did not deter my mother. When she had travelled to Germany, a German acquaintance of hers living in Northwich had travelled with her to visit her own family and they had arranged to return together. Her acquaintance had bought food delicacies not then available in England, such as jars of rollmop herrings and thin slices of meat in mayonnaise.

They took the train from Hamburg to Hook of Holland and then the overnight boat to Harwich. From there they would take the train to Manchester. Many British troops were on the ferry and on arriving at Harwich the customs were more than usually thorough in examining everyone's luggage. The soldiers were made to empty out their kitbags and the customs officers even opened the jars of food my mother's friend was carrying and stirred the contents looking for something.

My mother hung back until the last moment and then went up to one of the customs officers and said haughtily, "I hope this is not going to take much longer as my train is due to leave in two minutes." The customs officer replied, "Have you anything to declare?" to which she replied, "Of course not, I have only these two suitcases." The customs officer took his blue chalk, marked each case with a cross, and let her go to the train.

My father was excitable, quick to anger and quite nervous in some situations. My mother always said his nervousness was due to his time on the run from the Gestapo. He was also very clever, cultured, a great conversationalist, and very knowledgeable and passionate about horticulture. He became most nervous in front of people in uniform, particularly the police and postmen.

As an example, I remember one incident in probably 1962. By this time Queenie the Fox Terrier had died and we had acquired an eighteen-month-old Labrador called Skipper. The Labrador had been with a family who could not give it the attention it needed, and it was left alone in the garden for much of the day. Naturally, it found a way out and would, as most Labradors do, wander all over the place. Eventually the family realised they could not care for the dog. Fortunately, my parents knew them and agreed to take Skipper, as he could have the run of the nursery without causing a public nuisance.

We soon discovered that, as much as my father was frightened of people in uniform, Skipper hated them with an indescribable vengeance and would attack them ferociously if not held back. It was thought that he had been kicked badly by someone in uniform as a young dog and had ever since held a serious grudge.

One winter morning I was sitting having breakfast when the postman knocked, as he had a parcel to deliver. My father was just getting out of bed so I thought that, as the parcel would be for him and he would probably have to sign for it, he should answer the door. Naturally, Skipper immediately started to bark and tried to break through the door to get at the postman.

My father, who in winter got his night's sleep in short bursts, had gone to bed in a pair of old 'long johns' underpants (the waist elastic of which had either broken or not been tied properly). As he opened the door and took hold of Skipper to prevent the postman being torn to shreds, he had let go of his loose long johns and they began to fall — so revealing parts of him that he did not necessarily want the postman to see.

Having wedged the door open with his bare foot, and still holding on to the dog, he made a grab for his descending underpants, thus preserving his modesty. So far so good, but then the postman (not wanting to come too close for obvious reasons) stretched out his hand holding the parcel he wished to deliver. My father, forgetting his underpants, tried to reach the parcel but then realised his long johns were beginning to fall again. He therefore had to retrieve his hand from the parcel he was trying to reach and again make a quick grab for his falling underwear. By pulling them up very high and standing with his legs wide apart, he managed to reach the parcel, preserve his modesty and prevent the dog from tearing the postman apart.

The postman beat a hasty retreat and, because my father was standing with his legs wide apart, he did not have a lot of control over his forward balance. Skipper was by now a big, powerful dog and, seeing that the postman was leaving, realised that (although being held by my father) this was his last chance to get that pesky postman. The dog lunged and my father only just managed to prevent himself from being pulled out of the house and simultaneously losing his long johns.

Somehow, he managed get himself, the dog and the parcel inside the house without exposing himself. I was sitting at the breakfast table, laughing helplessly, and my mother (who had been in the kitchen) also came in and saw the funny side of the situation. My father was furious and began shouting, asking why we had not helped him. The dog crept away in a very disconsolate manner, having failed to seize the postman once again.

Like Queenie, Skipper always accompanied my father to the nursery but, having seen my father on to the premises, immediately disappeared — only returning in time to accompany my father back to the bungalow for lunch or the evening. Interestingly he remained with my father when he accompanied him on his winter nights' boiler-stoking visits.

Eventually we discovered where Skipper went in the mornings and afternoons, because I decided, while on school holidays, to take him for a walk one afternoon. I went with my father and Skipper to the nursery and then began to take the dog for a walk. Thinking how good he was at walking by my side I did not put him on the lead.

All went well until we walked past a bungalow, when suddenly he turned towards it and ran into the open door — and before I could catch him, he was coming out again, chasing the cat out of the house. He then returned inside and as I ran in to retrieve him, I saw that he was eating the cat's food; as I tried to pull him away, he refused to budge.

At that point the lady of the house came out of her living room. Surprised and ashamed, I let go of Skipper who, having devoured the cat's food, ran into the living room and lay down before the burning open fire. I apologised profusely to the woman and made to go into the living room to forcibly remove Skipper. She replied, "Oh, leave him — he does this every day except Sunday and keeps me company for an hour. As for eating the cat's food, it is only the leftovers and I would only have to throw it away." The woman went on to tell me that after an hour or so he left her and visited two other houses on West Park because he had his rounds to make. She also knew that in the morning he had a similar visiting routine on East Park.

The only time he varied his routine was when the local butcher came in his van to sell meat. As the butcher parked his van, women would form an orderly queue, which Skipper would join. As each person was served, the queue progressed so that the next person was served. Skipper, who had been sitting patiently between two prospective customers, would stand up and move up accordingly until he came to the butcher, who would always give him some scrap of meat and sometimes a bone he could not sell. I would not have believed this if I had not seen it with my own eyes.

As long as there were no policemen or postmen about, Skipper was a lovely placid dog — except when he saw another large dog with which he could fight (he then became ferocious). Quite early on, he had lost part of one of his ears and had scars all over his face. Once, he fought so hard that one of his fangs broke off about a quarter of an inch from the tip.

I mentioned to my father that, as the fang was hollow, if it was not filled it would become infected and would have to be removed. So, my father took Skipper to the local vet, who said the only solution was to extract the fang. My father asked if it could not be filled, to which the vet replied that he did not have the equipment, filling or the skill to perform such a process. My father was just about to agree to the extraction when the vet said that he had a friend who was a dentist and would call him immediately to see if he could perform the filling.

The dentist found the request very funny but agreed to come to the vet's as soon as his practice closed. The vet anaesthetised Skipper; the dentist then cleaned the inside of the fang with some of the vet's instruments and filled the hole with amalgam. Afterwards when people looked at Skipper they would often remark on his broken fang, to which we would say, "Yes, he has got a broken fang but we took him to a dentist who filled it." They would ask who the dentist was because they did not want to use a dentist that also treated animals. We would reply, truthfully, that we could not remember his name because the vet never told us.

My father could be very absent-minded, especially regarding putting his still smouldering pipe into his jacket pockets. For a while my mother would sew the holes in the side-pockets of his jacket that had been burnt from burning ash falling out of his pipe. In the end, she gave up and he had to resort to trying to sew them himself but, as he could never find a needle and thread, he would use wreath wire. On putting his hand into one of the jacket side-pockets he would often prick his hand on one of the sharp ends of the wire.

In summer, when not wearing a jacket, he would put his smouldering pipe into one of his trouser pockets, thus making holes in the pockets and sometimes burning his thighs. He always wore rubber boots, with his trousers tucked into the boots, because of the need to be constantly watering plants. This also had the benefit that when he put anything into his trouser pockets it fell down into one of his rubber boots. I can remember several times, when he needed to give change, he would take off one of his boots and pour out coins from it. How people felt receiving coins that had been around his feet is anyone's guess, but I never heard them complain.

The most amusing story I remember him telling me was about one hot summer's day when he was working outside with two of his employees putting plants in the ground. Wearing a shirt and trousers, he stood up and lit his pipe and took a few puffs. Then, for some inexplicable reason, instead of putting his pipe in one of his side pockets he put it in his back one and proceeded to bend down and continue planting.

Within seconds the smouldering ash had fallen out of the pipe, burning a hole in the pocket and then through his underpants, and finally coming to rest on the tender skin of his posterior. Feeling the effects of the burning ash on his bare skin, he leapt up from his bent position and, realising what he had done, attempted to do two things at once.

Firstly, to retrieve the pipe from his back pocket — but in his haste to take hold of it he managed to spill more burning ash down the back of his legs. Secondly, he ran in a jerky, hopping motion as quickly as he could to the nearest water tap in order to extinguish his now smouldering trousers and cool his burnt skin. The two workers found the whole incident so funny they fell about laughing, and a halt had to be called to the planting until they could compose themselves and my father had recovered from his burns.

Towards the end of 1954 the Ford V8 Estate started to exhibit problems with its brakes. This manifested itself one day when my father was driving down a steep hill. As my father descended the hill, he put his foot on the brakes (as there was a stop sign at the bottom of the hill) but nothing happened. Using the gears and hand brake he managed to slow the car down and fortunately, because there was nothing coming from the right at the stop sign, managed to turn to the left and pull in to the kerb, hence stopping the car.

I don't know whether he continued on to his destination or not but he very gingerly drove the van home, and in the evening rang John Aird to see if he could help. John said that his mechanic friend could fix the brakes very cheaply but as the man worked during the day, he could only do it at night, so would require the V8 for a week or so to do the repairs. My father explained to John that he needed a vehicle for his business and could not be off the road for so long. John explained that the mechanic had a 1918 Morris Post Office van that my father could use until the V8 was repaired.

The following Sunday John Aird came from Penketh to Marbury and left what I could only describe as a veteran vehicle with us, and drove away with the V8. How he too managed to drive the V8 without brakes remains a mystery. The film "Genevieve", about the veteran car rally from London to Brighton, had been released earlier in the year and so we christened the van Genevieve.

The Post Office van was an amazing vehicle. It was brown in colour with the letters GPO still visible. It stood at least six feet high. The windscreen was vertical and there was only one electric windscreen wiper and one seat on the driver's side. The gear stick and handbrake were long and upright, and the only instruments I can remember on the dashboard were the speedometer, ignition light and lights switch. The water temperature gauge sat on top of the external radiator filler cap at the front of the bonnet. It had a gravity-feed fuel system, which meant the fuel tank just in front of the windscreen sat above the top of the back of the engine, with the fuel pipe draining directly into the carburettor. The roof of the van sloped down over the driver's cab past the windscreen, making me think that perhaps originally there had been no windscreen or windscreen wiper. The only protection for the driver would then have been the sloping roof.

All went well for the first couple of days, then either my mother or father had to drive into Northwich. The drive to Northwich entailed descending a very steep hill called Soot Hill, with a very narrow bridge over the canal near the top of the hill (which in those days had a sharp right-hand turn) and, once over the bridge, a sharp left-hand turn.

The return journey from Northwich meant a steep ascent and negotiating the turns immediately before and after the bridge in reverse order. If that was not enough, as one ascended and saw a vehicle coming the other way that was already on the bridge, one had to stop on the steepest part of the hill, just before the bridge, and wait for the descending vehicle to pass.

This was challenging enough in an ordinary vehicle with a fuel pump. As my father or mother discovered, with a gravity-feed fuel system on a steep hill insufficient fuel would reach the engine and so it would not have sufficient power to start moving again.

The only solution was to roll back down the hill to a less steep part (hoping that there was no car behind), rev the engine (and hope nothing was coming down the hill at that moment), then drive back up the hill (as fast as one dared) round the sharp right- and left-hand bends, onto and off the bridge. When I accompanied my father to market, I always prayed on the way home that the Soot Hill Bridge would be clear. After a few weeks the V8's brakes were finally repaired and we could ascend Soot Hill safely again.

In 1955 or 1956 Herbert Fränkel decided it was time to leave London for a more agreeable tax haven. He had persuaded the UK immigration and tax authorities that he was only in the UK for a temporary period (until hostilities ended and he could find a more permanent home). As a result, he paid very little tax and managed to remain in the UK from about 1937 to 1955 without being disturbed.

However, in 1955 the tax authorities began to query why he was still in the UK and paying very little tax. He saw an advert for a large three-storey villa standing in an acre of ground on the outskirts of Geneva. He promptly bought it for one hundred thousand pounds and moved, rather hastily, to avoid further inquiries from Her Majesty's Inland Revenue. The building itself was in good repair but needed new bathrooms, some alterations and painting of both the interior and exterior.

Herbert decided he wanted the garden (of at least an acre) totally renovated. So, he asked my father to come to Geneva and redesign it. This meant my father flying there, which was totally unheard of in those days. I was so excited that someone from our family would fly on a commercial aeroplane that I boasted to all my friends about it (and to anyone else who would listen).

My mother and I drove him to Ringway Airport, Manchester. We went into a corrugated hut with red leather armchairs. There, a British European Airways person took his ticket for the first leg of his journey to London Heathrow, where he would change for the flight to Geneva.

Commercial air travel was, in those days, still in its infancy and I remember thinking: what if the plane crashes and he is killed — how will we manage? Just then I saw him walk up to a machine, into which he put four half crowns (ten shillings in total) and out came a printed card, on which he wrote something. He came over to my mother and gave her the card and said, "If I am killed during any of the four flights this card shows that my life is insured for ten thousand pounds." I was so relieved, because the amount was such a lot of money that it would take care of us for many years.

He returned home a few days later and, as much as I tried to get him to talk about the flights, he wanted to talk about how he had designed Herbert's garden. He flew to Geneva, at Herbert's expense, three or four times more before the garden was completed.

For the first years in Marbury we didn't have a summer holiday because there was not sufficient money, and my parents worked nearly every day to build the business. I was lucky because a Cub Scout Pack was formed in early 1955 and the cub and scout master, Mr Holland, organised a week in the summer at the chemical company's holiday camp in North Wales (at a place called Dyseth). Apart from that and the odd day trip to the seaside or into Derbyshire I don't remember any holidays until 1957.

Early in that year we visited John and Edith Aird, and after a while the conversation turned to the continental holiday we had had together in 1951, and how we had enjoyed it. All of a sudden, my father said, "Let's do it again." But nobody was keen to tour Germany and Austria again. Then my mother said, "I would like to visit the Mediterranean, particularly the French Rivera." The adults all agreed that that was what they would do.

By now my father had had to sell the V8 as it was nearly using more oil than petrol. He bought a small early-1950s Bedford van, which had just a front bench seat. John Aird said he knew where he could get it serviced very cheaply to ensure it would be fully roadworthy for a three-thousand-mile journey across France. Four old car seats were acquired and fittings made so that four people could sit in the back of the van, and windows were fitted along the sides to provide light and a view for the passengers in the rear.

At some stage, well before we were due to leave for our Mediterranean holiday, my father had to fly again to Geneva to work on Herbert's garden. While there he mentioned to Herbert that we planned to travel to the Mediterranean for our summer holiday. Herbert suggested we stop off and stay with him for a couple of days en-route in order that Herbert could meet Helen and me, and so that my father could see the garden in full bloom. Well, we were all very excited at the prospect. So, the plan was that we would first visit Paris for two days, then Geneva for a similar amount of time and finally drive to the South of France.

A couple of days before we were due to leave, John Aird came and picked up the Bedford van and took it to his mechanic friend for a full check and service before embarking on the journey. My mother had heard from someone how expensive accommodation was in France so she borrowed a six-person tent from the Marbury scout troop. On the Friday afternoon of our departure, John and Edith arrived with the freshly serviced van.

Everything was packed into it, including the large tent, and then we all climbed in and we set off from Marbury. We had only driven eleven miles and were just coming out of Middlewich, a town south of Northwich, when we heard a rumbling noise from one of the back wheels. Suddenly the van came to a screeching halt. We got out thinking we had a flat tyre but found instead that one of the back wheels had come off — but had fortunately got trapped under the rear mudguard, so was still holding the back axle off the road.

The van was jacked up to assess the damage, which in fact was very minor except that one of the five wheel nuts was missing and could not be found. A quick analysis came to the conclusion that when the mechanic had removed the wheel to check the brakes, he had not tightened the nuts when putting the wheel back. The van was already on its jack and the wheel was firmly secured in place with the four remaining nuts, and we set off again. A fifth wheel nut was not fitted until we returned to Marbury some three weeks later. On nearing London, John Aird took over the driving through London and on to Dover, where we caught the ferry to Calais.

From Calais we drove on to Paris. During the journey to Paris we became very impressed with the French motorcars, particularly the strange looking Citroen 2CV and the very futuristic spaceship-like Citroen D19, both of which handled the uneven French roads with ease.

On reaching Paris we found a cheap, very old-fashioned hotel for two or three nights. The only thing I can remember about the hotel was the mouthpiece of the telephone in the bedroom. It was just a tube to the earpiece, so when one spoke into it the earpiece acted like a microphone. The other thing was the man on reception, whom I heard speak in French — so I naturally assumed he was French, until he spoke to me in a strong northern English accent.

I also remember that soft drinks were so expensive I was only allowed to drink lukewarm Perrier water and one other similar water — both tasted foul to someone used to orange squash and Tizer. The two more memorable things were our parents taking Helen and myself to the Louvre art gallery, which Helen and my father enjoyed very much. All I wanted to see was the Mona Lisa, which I eventually did. The other thing I wanted to see was the Eiffel Tower, so my father took me, and when we got there, I wanted to take the lift to the top — but it cost the equivalent of ten shillings each. My father said we could not afford the money, so instead we walked up to the first floor of one of the four legs. It was such a thrill for me to stand on the viewing platform and look over Paris.

From Paris we drove to Geneva, where we met Uncle Herbert and Aunty Mary (as I was told to call her, even though, at the time, they were not married). We stayed in Uncle Herbert's villa at Pres de Lours. It appeared to me to be a palace with large spacious rooms, antique furniture and valuable oil paintings hanging on nearly every wall. It had three storeys and naturally we were put on the top floor with the cook. Herbert and Mary both had their bedrooms, bathrooms and, in Herbert's case, a large study, and in Mary's a private sitting room on the first floor.

Herbert had recently bought a new American Pontiac car. I don't think I had ever been in a new car before, and especially not a 1950s-style American car that one only saw on the television. I was delighted when he took me for a drive and let me sit in the front seat. To my surprise it did not have a manual gearbox like most British cars. I could not imagine how an automatic one worked.

The only other thing I remember was that at the last day's lunch, for dessert, there was a chocolate mousse covered with whipped cream and presented in a large glass bowl. There were six of us at the table (as the Airds were staying somewhere else). Mary spooned it into six individual glass bowls, which she handed out.

There was one portion remaining. It was delicious and, as I discovered much later in life, not made in the traditional way from egg yolks etc. but with evaporated milk. Of course, us greedy Franks were all hell bent on finishing our portion first so that one of us would get the last remaining portion. Just as we were racing to beat each other, Mary very cleverly and diplomatically said, "It is so good I think I will give cook the remaining portion so she can taste how good it is." Fortunately, my mother obtained the recipe from Mary and often made it.

Leaving Geneva, the plan had been to head for the South of France and the French Rivera. However, my parents and the Airds had not realised how expensive France was at that time compared with the UK. So, it was decided it would be cheaper to drive to the Italian Rivera and in particular a town called Bordighera, just a few miles over the French border in Italy. The plan was to drive down the Rhone valley and then into Italy, but unfortunately there had recently been heavy flooding and the road had been completely destroyed.

The only alternative was to take an old military road over the mountains, which we did. This proved much more difficult as it was a single-track road that in many parts was not asphalted. It was very steep with tight hairpin bends. The left-side of the road was in most places a rockface and the other, on which we drove, a sheer drop with no metal barriers for protection. It was a terrifying experience but the doughty Bedford van with its little 1200 cc side-valve engine kept on going upwards, mainly in first gear, with six people, their luggage and a large tent.

Fortunately, we did not encounter any serious problems until suddenly round a blind hairpin bend came a big truck occupying the width of the road. My mother, who was driving at the time, spotted an indentation in the rock wall on the left-hand side and illegally drove into it, as close as possible to the rock wall, and stopped and waited for the truck to pass to the right of us. Without hesitating the truck moved slowly forward very close to us, with the driver looking out of his window to see if the wheels remained on the road. As it passed, I looked behind to see the outside wheel of the rear double-wheels turning in space but it passed safely and went on its way.

The incident was talked about for many years to come, particularly how my mother had the foresight and downright cheek to pull onto the wrong side of the road. Finally, we reached a high plateau and drove through a deserted military barracks. The road led through the parade square, in the middle of which was a gallows, with the rope still hanging (but the noose had rotted-away).

We finally descended into Turin, where we stayed the night. Having found somewhere to stay, we went out to eat and found a somewhat dubious restaurant. I remember that John Aird ordered fish, which turned out to be a very thin flat fish. John, always wanting to be the life and soul of the party (forgive the pun), said, as he put his knife into the fish, "In a minute I will get to the middle of this fish!"

The next day we arrived in Bordighera and began to look for somewhere to stay. Initially we thought we would use the tent and so looked at a campsite. Then we realised that apart from the tent we had no other camping equipment, such as sleeping bags, cooking equipment or utensils, and no folding chairs on which we could sit. So, plan "B" was hurriedly initiated to look for accommodation.

Fortunately, we found a small bed-and-breakfast not very far from the beach. I can remember very little about it except for the fact that an Italian woman ran it and her husband was German, and it had a plant nursery at the back of it. He grew pelargoniums. My father soon got into conversation with him and the man gave him some cuttings, which my father wrapped in a polythene bag and put in the glove compartment of the van — and promptly forgot about them until we arrived home, where he cultivated the cuttings (which originated from three different varieties of the same plant). He renamed the three plant varieties Christine Frank, Helen Frank and Peter Frank.

The following day we set off for the beach. To my disappointment it was a steep pebble beach and the waves were large — hardly somewhere one could paddle or play in the sea. But my father showed us how to get into the sea by diving into a braking wave, swimming through it and surfacing on the other side, where the water was relatively calm but deep. He then showed us how to get out by waiting for a wave, then as it approached swimming as fast as possible in the direction of the shore and allowing the wave to carry one onto the beach. The only problem was that if you stopped swimming the wave would catch up with you, depositing you on the pebble beach in a very painful manner.

We spent the whole day on the beach. The sun was very strong, and we had neither an umbrella nor sun cream for protection. That night I had terrible sunburn. My mother managed to obtain some calamine lotion that helped. The next day I had to stay in bed until I had recovered.

It was during this time that my father and John Aird began to calculate how long it would take us to drive back to Calais, avoiding the Rhone by heading further west and then up through central France. They realised that what was meant to be a seaside holiday would actually mean we could only stay four days by the sea before beginning our return journey (one of which I spent in bed with sunburn).

I can only remember three other things during our four-day Mediterranean seaside holiday. Firstly, the sea was a stunning azure colour. Secondly, my sister met an Italian boy who came every evening to meet her. While waiting for her to come out he serenaded her (and us) with Italian songs. Lastly, my mother allowed me to buy a small flick-knife costing eleven hundred Italian lira (about one pound). Flick-knives had recently been declared illegal in the UK so I felt very daring. As soon as we arrived home, I put it in a drawer and left it there until five years later when I sold it to a boy in my class.

After four days beside the sea we set off westwards along the coast road to Monaco, where we stopped in Casino Square of Monte Carlo. I remember looking at the casino and the Hotel de Paris, which overlooked the square, thinking I would never be rich enough to visit the casino or stay in the hotel. We climbed back into the van and drove on to Nice and from there to Avignon.

After that I can remember nothing of the rest of our return journey to Calais except my mother, who was very proud of her tan, saying that she was going to wear a dress that plunged at the back to show off her tan. I asked what happened if it was very cold when we arrived in Calais. She replied that in that case she would very loosely drape a cardigan over her shoulders, which would slip a little way down her back to show off her tan.

We arrived at the port and it was cold and blowing a gale. On getting out of the car on the boat and climbing up to the passenger deck, she buttoned up her cardigan to her neck in order to keep warm — so sadly nobody could see her tan. On reaching Dover we drove home and so ended the second and last great European adventure with the Airds.

We remained good friends with them for many years but, as often happens, contact grew less and less until one day in the 1970s John Aird called to say Edith had died. I don't know how often after that that my parents met John. I only know that my sister remained in contact with him until the 1980s or 1990s, when he too died.

As a footnote to our visit to Casino Square in Monte Carlo, twenty years later I was awarded, along with other salespeople, a trip to Monte Carlo. I stayed in the Hotel Paris: the balcony of the bedroom overlooked the square and I spent the first evening in the casino.

Chapter 11

Business Growth and the Sports Saloon

In the previous March (of 1957) I had sat my eleven-plus examination, which determined whether one was allowed to attend grammar school. I was convinced I had failed. Firstly, because on writing my name on the examination papers I did not know how to spell Edmund (my third name). Sometimes my parents said it was Edmund and sometimes Edmond. This, I learned much later, was because my paternal grandfather's mother was French and, although he was christened Edmund, she pronounced it Edmond. Secondly, while having lunch between the examinations a boy sitting opposite me remarked that I had crossed my knife and fork, which was a sign of bad luck and I would therefore fail. Of course, I never told my parents anything about the whole day and, if they asked, I just replied as usual, "It was all right."

One Friday morning in May as I got on the school bus, a boy excitedly said he had passed. I, having totally put out of my mind the exam because I was so sure I had failed, asked him what he had passed. He then told me that a letter had arrived that morning informing his parents that he had been successful in getting into grammar school. I was very pleased for him but thought about how disappointed my parents would be when they read about my result. Having been told many times that I was stupid, I just accepted my lot and got on with life.

On arrival in class at school several others knew their results, but many didn't (such as myself). Fortunately, the teacher had a list of the passes and failures and began to read it out. Imagine my surprise and pleasure when my name was read out as having passed! But it was so sad for the children who had not passed — some were crying and others just looked totally down-trodden, as though they had (at the age of eleven) been rejected by society. The saddest situation was a boy and girl who were twins: the girl passed and the boy failed.

The teacher spent the rest of the morning trying to restore confidence and some sense of self-worth in those who had not passed. I just sat in a complete dream, thinking how pleased my parents would be and what a relief it was that I had somehow managed to pass — despite having possibly misspelled my third Christian name and having crossed my knife and fork, and that there would be no hand-wringing and sack-cloth-and-ashes for weeks afterwards at home.

Unlike most of the parents of my friends, my parents (having come from Central and Eastern Europe and themselves both attended the equivalent of grammar school — and had matriculated) fully understood the value of education. As a further example of how important education was for the Central and Eastern Europeans friends of my parents, a year or two later the son of the Polish lady who had the continental food stall opposite my parents stall on the Saturday market told me, with tears in her eyes, that her son had not passed the eleven-plus examination. She was distressed the whole day.

Many of the other parents whose children didn't pass would have just forgotten about it and thought: well, so their child would go to the local Secondary Modern (what a terrible name for the alternative to Grammar School) and, because there was almost full employment at the time, the child would get a job on leaving at fifteen years old.

A week or so later my parents and I had to attend an interview with the headmaster of the grammar school. The only thing I can remember being asked by the headmaster was what was my weakest subject, and I replied, "Spelling." With that he asked me to stand up and look out of the window and try to line-up two trees in the distance, first with one eye and then the other. I can't remember if I was able to or not, but he explained to my parents that some very early research was showing that children who could not line up distant objects with one or the other eye had the potential to be poor at spelling.

Many years later I met a woman who suffered badly, as did her children, from dyslexia. She explained that she had no leading-eye and found it impossible to write properly and in straight lines. I related my experience at the headmaster's interview and she immediately understood why the headmaster had been trying to assess whether I had a leading-eye.

On returning home from our European holiday there was a large envelope awaiting us from the grammar school, explaining in great detail all the uniform and sports clothes my parents had to buy for me. By the age of eleven I was already a very big person. So big that most of my uniform, particularly the blazer and grey flannel trousers, had to be tailor-made for me. It must have cost my parents a fortune but for them it was worth it — their son had got into grammar school and that was all that mattered.

I began at Sir John Deane's Grammar School in September 1957. Soon after I began, I had to attend the orthopaedic clinic in Northwich for a regular check on the progress of how my legs were straightening, as a result of the operations two years earlier. On examination the doctor said that my legs had straightened and the metal plates should now be removed. Later in September a letter came saying I was to be admitted to the Robert Jones and Agnes Hunt orthopaedic hospital in Oswestry, late in October, to have the plates removed. We were told that this was a very straightforward procedure and I would be in hospital for less than two weeks.

About the same time, my mother had agreed to attend grandfather Blaschke's eightieth birthday party in Germany. To shorten the time that she would be away it was decided that she would fly rather than take the train and boat. We took my mother to Ringway Airport in Manchester sometime in the last week of October; it was half-term week so I was able to go with my father to the airport to see her off.

On the Sunday my father took me to Oswestry hospital for what was supposed to have been a relatively short stay. I remember my mother coming to visit me after her return from my grandfather's birthday celebrations. When her mother died in February 1950 in Warburton, she left a very old-fashioned black Persian lamb coat, which my mother would occasionally wear on very cold winter days. She took it with her to Germany where her father noticed how old-fashioned it looked and paid to have it remodelled in the style of the early 1960s. When she came to visit me at Oswestry the Sunday after she returned, I was lying on my bed outside the ward. She was wearing the remodelled coat and I could not get over how glamorous she looked.

As with the first time in hospital, there were complications and I ended up being in hospital for over five weeks and I had to learn to walk again. I finally left hospital in early December and still needed some time at home to fully recuperate.

Once home I was still very weak and tired easily even though I had walking sticks for support. One day, as a change from lying at home all day alone, my mother suggested I could drive with her to North Wales to collect Christmas trees that were to be sold on the market. First, we drove to Pentrevoeilas to see Ruth, the wife of my godfather Dai, for a short while, then we had lunch in the local pub where, even on a weekday, they served a delicious roast dinner with soup and a dessert for about five shillings.

We then went to the place from where my father had ordered the Christmas trees. As we drove into what looked like a very muddy farmyard there was no one about. However, there was a short, steep and very muddy track leading down to a barn where my mother thought the Christmas trees would be. So, she drove down to find there was nobody there either. My mother got out of the van and went to look for somebody.

She finally returned with the foreman who, in a Welsh accent, said that only tractors drive down to the barn and that the trees were in a barn in the yard above. Without showing any concern my mother got back into the van and drove up the muddy track, without any problems, to where the Christmas trees were. With the trees loaded, we set off on our return journey, during which I begged my mother to drive via Oswestry hospital. This she did, so that I could take one last look at the hospital where I had spent over thirteen weeks of my life.

Finally, in December (two weeks before the end of term) our GP agreed that I could go back to school. But I still could not ride my bicycle to school, so my parents took me each day in the van. The teachers all welcomed me back but asked why I had bothered to come back for the last two weeks of term.

In the mid-1950s the Vauxhall Car Company, which made the Bedford trucks and vans, had introduced a van that was almost flat-fronted, had sliding driver and passenger doors, a more powerful overhead-valve engine and increased load-space. My father desperately wanted one but could not afford the cost, until one day in about May 1958 he heard that someone was selling one second-hand at a price he could afford.

He bought it and I remember my mother and I driving home with him in it. There was a driver's seat and a passenger seat for two people. He was very proud that he had managed to acquire such a vehicle. As we drove home to Marbury, I remember my father saying that a couple of years ago he had said that within five years of setting up in business he would have one of these vans, as it was a sign of his business becoming more successful. He went on to say that within another five years he would have a Jaguar. He never realised that dream but did have a different type of sports saloon, but more of that later.

Our two-week summer holiday in 1958 was spent in Devon. We found a bed-and-breakfast in Dartmouth. My parents spent much of the time looking up old friends and acquaintances from the time when they had lived there. They showed us where they had been married and the then derelict cottage in which they had lived.

My most memorable day was the Plymouth Royal Navy Day, when we were allowed to walk onto various warships in port. I had become an avid reader of war-at-sea books and was desperate to get into a front-gun-turret and pretend I was sinking ships with my dead-eyed aim. Imagine my disappointment when, on trying to get into one of the turrets, I found I was already (at the age of twelve) too big to climb into it. I could merely look in while other normal sized boys could enter with ease. The other thing we did, on days when it was not cold and raining, was go to Torbay beach and swim in the cold sea. It was, to say the least, invigorating, unlike the warmth of the Mediterranean the previous year.

It was during this holiday that, while we were eating dinner in a restaurant, I burped loudly. My mother was horrified and told me off for doing so. She then said to my father, "Henry, please tell Peter how much you disapprove of what he has just done." My father, who at that moment was (for some reason) in an obdurate mood, replied to my mother, "Why should I, when he can burp better than I can." Actually, instead of using the word "burp" he used the German word "rülpsen", which my parents used instead of burp or belch. When I was young, I thought "rülpsen" was an English word; it was only later that I learned the words "burp" or "belch".

At home my father often burped, and my mother would immediately say the German word "Mahlzeit", which I thought was some kind of admonishment. Privately, my mother would explain to me that it was very impolite to burp but exused my father because he supposedly had a delicate stomach.

Roll forward many years from then and I am living in Austria. At the beginning of a meal people say to each other, "Mahlzeit". At first, I thought to myself, "Why? Nobody has burped." I soon discovered that it literally means a meal or mealtime but is used in the context similar to saying in English "eat well" or in French "bon appétit". I further discovered that "Mahlzeit", used as an expression in German slang means "that's great" or "that's just great". So, I finally understood my mother's admonishing and sarcastic use of the word "Mahlzeit".

Scout camp that summer was near the south Lake District village of Silverdale. We travelled by train, changing somewhere to a local service to reach Silverdale. The tents and all our kitbags had been taken by lorry. What we did not know was that the campsite was quite a march from the train station, and it was raining.

We walked for what seemed to be an hour and, on reaching the farm where our campsite was, it was discovered that the lorry had been delayed and had only just arrived so our tents had not been erected, and we had to wait in a barn (which was at least dry). Finally, we were told our tents were ready and we could collect our kitbags and settle into our tents.

There was not a day during that week when it did not rain. The situation got so bad there was talk among the scout masters of abandoning the camp and returning home, but fortunately it did not happen and we held out under very wet conditions for the week.

On returning to school in September 1958 I made friends with a couple of boys who, one Saturday, took me to Crewe mainline station, train-spotting. I had no idea what this entailed and was none-the-wiser at the end of day, except that it was still in the days of the steam locomotive and I was covered in a grime of coal dust and soot from head to foot.

During school that year I became very interested in history because of an enthusiastic teacher. This interest has remained with me to this day. Also, I will never forget a religious knowledge lesson where I turned to the boy behind me and, for a prank, emptied his fountain pen over his exercise book.

The teacher, who was having trouble controlling the class, saw what had happened and came to me and started to hit me around the head. It seemed to go on forever as he screamed at me, "Why did you empty the pen on his exercise book?" I looked at one of my friends sitting at the desk next to me, silently pleading with him to ask the teacher to stop hitting me. Eventually he stopped and my head rang for the rest of the day. The beating will remain in my memory forever. Coincidentally, the teacher left the school at the end of the school year.

We didn't have a family holiday in 1959. I spent a week at scout camp on a farm near Nevyn on the Llŷn Peninsula in North Wales. The camp was only a couple of minutes from the beach and as the weather was warm and sunny, we spent most of the week on the beach.

The farmer had a very large prize bull, which he led out into the field everyday where we were camped. The farmer gently pulled the bull along with a rope through the ring that was attached to the bull's nose. Our scoutmaster had told us that the bull could be very dangerous and we must not go near it. Having seen the bull we fully understood what he meant: it was huge. As an extra safety measure one of the farm workers always accompanied the farmer with a pitchfork in hand in case anything untoward happened.

Towards the end of the week I got some form of chill or infection, which appeared to pass after a good night's sleep and a couple of aspirins. But on reaching home I developed a bad ear infection. The doctor was called and prescribed a course of penicillin injections.

In those days the district nurse would come with a metal and glass syringe and a small bottle of penicillin. The bottle was sealed with a rubber cap, into which the nurse would insert the needle of the syringe and draw off the antibiotic. I was always terrified of the whole procedure — so much so that one day I tensed up so much after the nurse had stuck the needle in me, she couldn't push the plunger downwards to inject me.

Finally, I cried in pain and this relaxed me, allowing her to get the penicillin into me.

During my time in bed my parents had decided to redecorate the bungalow and to buy a second-hand refrigerator. It had a small ice tray so we could have cold drinks. The reason my parents decided on the renovations was because Uncle Jupp and Aunt Waldtraut were going to visit us.

They had driven over from Hamburg with grandfather Blaschke, Karl-Heinz and Hildegard to collect Brigitte, who had been with an English family in Cookham in the county of Berkshire in order to improve her English. They then planned to visit us in Cheshire for a couple of days. I was very excited at the thought of seeing Karl-Heinz again but when they arrived, he spent most of his time talking to my parents, explaining to them that he had had to get married because he had got his girlfriend pregnant.

They arrived with another couple who were in their own car and were friends of Waldtraut and Jupp. Except for Grandpa Blaschke there was obviously no room for them to stay in our tiny bungalow. So, my father arranged for them all to stay at the Grey Parrot Club between Winnington and Northwich. It was decided that Grandpa was to sleep in Helen's bed in the bedroom I shared with her, and Helen would sleep in the living room on what we called the studio couch.

When they arrived, they all came into our home and although they did not say anything, they appeared to be amazed at how small it was. Outside, a small crowd (mainly of men) gathered around the two German cars, admiring both the Mercedes-Benz 180 of Uncle Jupp and the Opel Rekord of their friends — cars the like of which had never before been seen on Marbury Park.

All the men remarked on the quality and finish of the cars. After giving our visitors lunch, consisting of some cold cuts of continental sausage and cheese with bread bought from the Polish lady's stall on the market, my mother and father guided them to their accommodation.

Because there was no way we could serve a meal to eight extra people, my father booked and paid for all of us to have dinner at the Grey Parrot for the two or three nights they stayed there. The Grey Parrot Club was the poshest hotel and restaurant in Northwich in the late 1950s. I was very excited, as I had never been inside before.

My grandfather said he was tired and decided not to come to dinner, but instead had a bit more of the bread and cold meats for his evening meal. My parents, Helen and I went off to the club in our best clothes, which for me was a white school shirt, over which I wore a light beige sweater, and my school trousers and shoes. The three-course dinner was, for me, a grand affair, with a special table having been made up for the eleven of us — with grown-ups and Karl-Heinz at one end (all speaking German) and Helen, Brigitte, Hildegard and myself at the other (speaking English).

The evening ended about 9.30 p.m. and we drove home, leaving the visitors to, as I thought, a night of luxury. On arrival at home my mother insisted I went straight to bed. She came in to say goodnight. Grandpa was already asleep in the other bed and as my mother bent down to kiss me goodnight, he let out a very large fart. My mother thought I had done it and was just starting to admonish me when I explained that I had not farted and pointed to the slumbering grandfather, who at that moment let out another thunderous evacuation of gas. My mother, wanting to defend him, made excuses for her father — explaining that he was very old and could not help himself while sleeping.

Sometime in early 1960 my father felt the business was doing well enough for us to afford a family car as well as the van. At first, he thought of buying a Jaguar and a friend of ours knew of someone wanting to sell a Jaguar saloon. It was arranged that the vendor would drive to the nursery early one evening so that my father could see the car. When the car arrived, my father took one look at it and asked the owner what year it was built. When he heard that it was first registered in 1937, he told the person he did not want it even though it was available for 75 pounds. I have often thought that if my father had bought the 1937 Jaguar saloon and kept it in good condition, what would it have been worth twenty years later?

My parents, particularly my father, did not give up on the idea of having a sports saloon; the question was, what was available in their price range that was not too old? My father started to buy the "Exchange and Mart", a weekly publication that sold everything one could think of, especially cars. Looking through the "cars for sale" section, which covered many pages, my father noticed that there were cars called Allards for sale at reasonable prices.

The Allard was the invention, or more likely the development, of a man called Sydney Allard, who wanted a car that would win the London to Monte Carlo Rally, which it did successfully in 1952. It was built in very small production quantities in Allard's factory, south of London.

It was about seventeen-foot-long and had a Ford V8 side valve engine, a three-speed gear box, leaf-spring suspension and most importantly a Miles Hourglass steering box (so-called because the actual steering mechanism looked like an hourglass). This was one of the most important features of the car because it meant one could turn the front wheels lock-to-lock in one turn of the steering wheel. This was a great advantage when driving over the Alpine roads, where one had to handle the many hairpin bends at speed. The body was made from aluminium: the weight of the car was in the chassis and the V8 engine, which ensured stability at speed and especially on the hairpin bends. There were two versions of the car. One was an open sports car, which had a very small, cramped rear bench seat, and the other a sports saloon that had more room for the rear passengers.

The problem was that because the car was produced in south London and in small quantities there were very rarely any second-hand ones available in the north west of England, and if one did become available locally it was outside my parents' price range.

Then one day we noticed a sports saloon for sale about twelve miles away for the low price of around ninety pounds. My father rang the number in the advertisement, and it was still for sale. So, my mother and father and I went to see it. It was in a bit of a sorry state. The radiator grill was missing and had been replaced by some metal mesh, and also the bodywork was shabby. It still had its original colours of yellow up to the windows and black above, but time had not been kind to the paintwork.

My father took it for a drive and realised it required mechanical work and a re-spray but decided, because it was so cheap, to buy it and have the necessary work done. On driving it home he realised there were more problems than he originally thought. The first thing to happen was a flat tyre. As we changed the wheel, he realised that what he had seen as new tyres on the car were actually bald ones into which a tread had been cut (in some places down to the canvas). Having changed the wheel, a mile or two later the car ran out of petrol so my mother, who was driving our Bedford van, had to find a petrol station still open and buy petrol to get the car home.

Once home the car was put into the lean-to glasshouse, where it received a complete overhaul from a Polish mechanic who lived in Hall. It was sprayed a light-green colour and the metal mesh radiator grill was painted with aluminium paint. The car looked very good, as it should have done, for all the money spent on it, including the new tyres.

Chapter 12

Germany and Switzerland, the Need for Speed, and Sailing

In spring 1960 my mother heard from her sister Waldtraut in Hamburg that Grandfather Blaschke had contracted stomach cancer and did not have very long to live. My parents decided that, as the Allard was now overhauled, we should drive to Allesberg in Germany, where he lived, to see him for the last time.

In September 1959 my sister Helen had begun a three-year hotel management and catering course at Courtfield College in Blackpool. In the summer of 1960, she wanted to get some European experience in the discipline. My mother had a schoolfriend who lived in a place called Bad-Mergentein, which had a small hotel. The schoolfriend knew the owner. In return for getting Helen a summer job in the hotel, she wanted her eldest son to spend the summer holidays in England to improve his English. So, as a quid-pro-quo, the schoolfriend arranged for Helen to get a summer placement at the hotel and we would take the son (called Ernst-Walter) back to England with us.

In July we set off in the Allard for Germany. Once on the German autobahn my father managed to reach one hundred miles an hour — the fastest I had ever been in a car. We arrived in Allesberg two days later to find Uncle Jupp, Aunt Waldtraut, Brigitte and Hildegard there. Grandpa Blaschke was by this time so ill he was bedridden. We spent a few days in Allesberg saying our last tearful goodbyes to Grandpa.

Leaving Allesberg we then set off for Bad Mergentein, where we spent a few more days getting Helen settled in and collecting Ernst-Walter. We then drove to Switzerland, where we planned to stay a couple of days with Uncle Herbert and Auntie Mary in Geneva. During the drive from Germany into Switzerland we drove over several mountain-passes with numerous hairpin bends. The design of the Allard came into its own with its combined power, long wheelbase and the Miles Hourglass steering box all making easy work of the steep inclines and hairpin bends.

On the way to Geneva we stopped in Interlaken to experience the Jung Frau Joch railway, which is mainly a tunnel climbing up the inside of the north wall of the Eiger Mountain to a glacier at about eleven-thousand feet. The journey was breathtaking, especially when the train stopped at one point, where one could alight and look out of a window onto the north face. But even more spectacular was the top station on the glacier, where one could hire skis, which my parents did and gingerly skied for the first time in over twenty years. Of course, I too had to try to ski but just kept falling over.

The one thing I learnt from my father that day was how to stand up again having fallen over while wearing skis. We were on the glacier under a bright blue sky and strong sun for at least four or five hours without any sun protection. I still felt all right on the way down and over dinner that evening, but as I went to bed my face began to burn. Ernst-Walter, with whom I was sharing a room, recommended that I apply a well-known German skin cream to my face. It immediately gave me relief so that I slept through the night. Little did I know that the cream contained water.

The next morning, I woke up and looked in the mirror and did not recognise my face — it was swollen like a football. The water from the cream had seeped through the outer layer of my facial skin and caused it to blister. I looked horrendous. On going down to breakfast, my parents were horrified. My father became very cross, first with me for having applied the cream and secondly with Ernst-Walter, whom my father thought should have known better about advising me to apply the cream.

That day, we drove to Geneva and I felt very unwell. It took several days for the blisters to burst and much longer for all the dead skin to finally peel away from my face. When we left Geneva en-route for our channel port my father decided to take a detour via Lake Annecy.

When we arrived at the lake it was a pleasant, warm sunny day so we decided we would swim. Then I noticed sailing dinghies for hire and persuaded my father to take me sailing. He did not need much persuading for, although he had not sailed since he was last in St. Gilgen ten years earlier, it was to him like riding a bicycle. He was immediately at home on the water.

We could only hire the boat for an hour as we still had to drive through much of France to get near to the channel port, from where we were due to cross the channel. When the hour was nearly up my father headed for the mooring and explained to me that I should take the mooring line and crawl up onto the front of the dinghy so that I would be able to tie it to one of the upright posts on the pontoon.

On reaching the mooring, one of the boat hire employees came to help us and initially held the stern so that my father could step onto shore. I was having difficulty tying the painter to the post. Without thinking, the employee ran to help me — letting go of the stern just as my father was stepping off the boat. Of course, as he stepped off the rear of the boat it drifted away from the pontoon and my father (luckily only wearing swimming trunks) dropped into the water, which came over his head. He had in his hands his three essentials: his pipe, his tin of tobacco and his Ronson Variflame Lighter. He went down into the water until only the top of his head could be seen under the surface — and he gripped the three items for dear life.

By this time the employee had secured the bow to the mooring and, hearing the splash, ran to see what had happened. As my father surfaced the employee asked in French if my father could swim, to which my father replied, "Non" then rolled on to his back, put the pipe into his mouth and blew out the water just like Popeye. He then swam backstroke to the shore, still gripping his tin of tobacco in one hand and his lighter in the other. As he climbed ashore the pipe was still in his mouth, the tobacco remained dry in its tin and the lighter soon dried in the sunshine. We arrived home a couple of days later with a great story to tell.

The rest of the summer holidays involved me going to scout camp in Rhyl, North Wales, for a week, Ernst-Walter returning to Germany and my one and only attempt to become an entrepreneur. A year or so earlier my father had acquired a large load of horse manure and had produced a good cash crop of mushrooms. I thought I would do the same. I had little idea of how to do it so I talked to my father about the idea. He explained that mushrooms thrive best on horse manure, which is normally expensive to buy. He had been lucky as he managed to get a load for only the transport costs.

He told me that mushrooms could be grown less successfully on pig manure and as there was a small pig farm next to the nursery, he would talk to the owner to see how much a load would cost. The owner was only too happy to let me have as much as I wanted because he had problems disposing of it.

My father then pointed out that the manure had to be forked and turned at least three times and then spread out in an empty part of the lean-to vinery. He asked who was going to do this. I asked a couple of boys from my school if they wanted some summer work, to which they agreed, and I agreed a deal with my father that he would pay the boys and purchase the mycelium (which would produce the mushrooms when planted in the manure) as I harvested the mushrooms and sold them on the market, and I would pay him back from the money I made.

The two boys and I started work on the pile of manure, effectively turning the heap inside out three times over a period of about two weeks. The weather was hot and sunny, and the pig manure smelled awful. The heap was then left to rest for a week or so and then spread on the floor of the vinery.

The mycelium was purchased and planted into what was now very dry manure, and covered with a layer of soil. Then we waited and waited and in total I managed to harvest five or six mushrooms. I suffered my first and only crop failure. I had no means of repaying my father so he very kindly let me off my debt.

On 26th August 1960 my mother received a telephone call from Allesberg telling her that Grandpa Blaschke had died. My mother flew to Germany for the funeral.

The rest of 1960 is a blank for me except that my parents became close friends with the lady who ran the Polish food stall on the market, to the extent that they took her on holiday several times (because she was a single parent). They remained friends with her for the rest of their lives.

Similarly, they met a German couple who also lived in Northwich. Their first names were Peter and Else. He had a square, eastern European face and square chest and was not particularly tall. His wife was tall and slim. Both spoke English but with accents. He was originally from Berlin and had come to England as a prisoner of war.

In the prisoner-of-war camp Peter was told that if he joined the British army bomb disposal squad he would be released from where he was being held. Presumably he was supposed to carry out the most dangerous parts of bomb disposal. Originally, he had trained in Berlin as a book-keeper, and on joining the bomb disposal squad found there was a similar position that had not been filled. He applied and got the position and so spent the rest of the war in relative safety. By the time my parents met them, Else was a cook in one of the chemical company's canteens. Peter was employed by a local chartered accountant. We often visited them, and them us, in the early 1960s. The most memorable thing I remember about him was that he always pronounced the word "know" as "now".

Now we have to return to my mother's love of freshwater fish. One of our neighbours was a very keen angler and fished at every opportunity in Marbury mere. One day, my mother saw him carrying a large fish home and asked what it was. He told her it was a pike and if cooked thoroughly made very good eating. Given my mother's love of lake fish she asked the man if ever he caught another such pike, she would gladly pay him for it. A week later he knocked on the door holding an even larger pike. That weekend Else and Peter had been invited for Sunday tea. My mother instantly thought the cooked pike would be the centrepiece of the table.

The couple arrived and sometime later a substantial afternoon tea was set out on the table, with the cooked pike as centre stage. It looked magnificent. We sat down to eat at the table, with my father as usual grumbling that lake fish was the main course of the meal. My mother served it with potato salad in mayonnaise and chopped onions, which I love. In Austria, potato salad is served in a vinegar and oil marinade.

My father grudgingly ate the pike, complaining all the way through the meal. I don't think Peter enjoyed it very much but in order not to disappoint my mother he ate it steadily, with my mother continually asking Else if she thought Peter was enjoying the pike. Else replied, "Oh don't worry Chris, if Peter is not enjoying it, he will tell you so." I think

Peter was just being polite. It was the one and only time I remember my mother serving pike.

The last time I remember seeing Else and Peter was one Sunday afternoon when they visited us and had just bought their first car. On leaving, he got into the car to drive away and drove into a tree. Fortunately, they were not hurt but the car was badly damaged.

In 1961 my parents were beginning to feel that the Allard was not fast enough for them but could not afford another, faster sports car. Then my father read in a car magazine that there was the possibility of installing an overhead valve conversion unit, which would increase the power of the car. Further research showed it was not possible to do the conversion on the standard Ford V8 side-valve engine, only on the V8 Mercury engine. Eventually such an engine and conversion unit were found, and work began on removing the current engine and installing the Mercury engine with the Dryden overhead valve conversion unit.

Numerous problems were overcome, all at additional cost. Eventually the car appeared ready. The engine compartment looked fabulous with its chrome-plated rocker box covers and twin SU carburettors, and it sounded like a real sports car. There was only one problem: the oil pressure remained stubbornly and dangerously low. Further research was undertaken only to find that after all the previous expense a special high-pressure oil pump still needed to be fitted. This was the last straw and my father decided to cut his losses and refit the old engine and sell the Mercury engine complete with its Dryden overhead valve conversion unit.

This was done just in time for our 1961 summer holiday in Geneva to stay with Uncle Herbert and Aunt Mary for two weeks. At our first dinner with Uncle Herbert and Aunt Mary it came out that my father had written to Herbert the previous summer to tell him of my mushroom business. Herbert immediately asked me if I had been successful and I was about to explain that I had suffered a crop failure when my mother said, "It was not a great success but at least he made enough money to pay Henry back." I was completely flabbergasted and said no more for the whole meal. My mother never did explain why she told the lie.

During the holiday, I persuaded my father to take me dinghy sailing on Lake Geneva, which we did several times and, although there was not much wind, I thoroughly enjoyed it. My mother would drive with us to where the boats were hired on the lake and would sit and watch us from the shore. I think she enjoyed the peace and quiet and the opportunity to rest from all her normal pressures and stresses of being a mother, wife, housewife — as well as contributing her fair share of work to the business.

I would like to add a footnote to my mushroom-growing saga. Later in 1961, because my father had not had any use for the space in the vinery, the manure was never removed. So, some eighteen months after the manure had been planted with mycelium, mushrooms began to appear in reasonable quantities. My father harvested the mushrooms and sold them on the market. He offered me the money from the sales but I insisted he kept it to pay for the wages of the boys who had helped me, and for the mycelium.

Our Geneva holiday came to an end and we set off for the channel coast port of Calais. We stayed somewhere overnight and the next day we drove through a town not far from Calais. My mother was driving and the traffic was fairly heavy. To drive slowly through a town where one drove on the right in a right-hand drive car was a privilege for my mother, instead of looking at the traffic ahead, she relied on my father to advise her of any problems ahead, such as the vehicle in front braking or traffic lights.

The problem was that my father was colour blind, particularly on red. He sat in the front passenger seat with his pipe either in his mouth or in his hands, together with his tin of Three Nun tobacco and his Ronson Varaflame gas lighter, continually saying, "Chris what are you doing? There is traffic ahead." My mother would reply, "I am window shopping — you watch the traffic, this is my only opportunity to look at the shops because you don't like too." Suddenly my father spotted traffic lights and cried out, "Chris, there are traffic lights ahead", to which my mother replied "What colour are they?" My father replied, "I can't tell", at which point I, sitting in the back seat, interjected, "They are red." My mother immediately braked.

We crawled through the town with the Allard's big V8 motor burbling away happily at low revs. Suddenly we passed a hardware shop and in the window my mother saw three matching saucepans of increasing size. They were covered in red enamel on the outside and white on the inside, with black enamel lids — a typical French design of the late fifties and early sixties. My mother exclaimed that she had never seen such beautiful and elegant saucepans. In England the only ones on offer were made of aluminium and turned a horrible grey colour once used.

She immediately proclaimed she wanted them, to which my father said, "No, we have already spent too much on this holiday — I am not spending another penny on non-essentials." My mother began to cry, saying, "You never let me have anything nice for the house, and deny me every pleasure in life!" This was not exactly true but her tears and ability to lay guilt on my father at the appropriate time made him relent and agree to buy the saucepans.

We stopped and walked back to the shop. Because my father spoke French, he had to transact the purchase. They cost about five pounds, a fortune for saucepans in 1961. They were packed in a brown cardboard box. My mother carried the box out of the shop looking radiant, triumphant and victorious. My father followed behind looking defeated, down-trodden and peeved.

To try and take the edge off my mother's pleasure he said, "We will have to pay duty on them at the Dover Customs." My mother turned to him and, in her most regal manner, said "We will not declare them — I will smuggle them into the country." Being the inveterate smuggler, she had no fear of Her Majesty's Customs Officers. My father, always terrified of uniformed authority (stemming from his time on the run from the Gestapo) winced, went white and hung his head in fear.

We returned to the car and drove to Calais to take the night boat to Dover. Although, even in those days, only a couple of hours sea voyage at most, the night ferry left Calais and anchored in the channel. Having booked a cabin, we would be able to sleep for at least five or six hours and have breakfast on board before arriving in Dover.

We arrived early in Calais so instead of waiting around at the port it was decided we should have one last meal in France. Having found a restaurant, we entered and were shown to a table by the maître d'. As we were eating our meal my father, who had been surprisingly quiet, suddenly said, "Well Chris, I hope you will bring the children when you visit me in prison?" My mother and I looked at each other in total surprise. She immediately said, "What are you talking about?", to which he replied, "Because when we get caught smuggling the saucepans, I will have to take responsibility and therefore will go to jail." Even I thought a jail sentence for smuggling three French saucepans costing five pounds was an exaggeration. My mother immediately retorted, "Don't be ridiculous."

At this point a row began to develop between them over the saucepans. I was fifteen, a very big awkward teenager with frizzy red hair that looked and felt like a mass of copper wire. No amount of Brylcreem would get it to lie flat so I could not look like one of the pop stars of the day. I was already embarrassed by my own presence, never mind my parents having a fully-fledged row in a French restaurant.

To quieten them down I suggested we explain our problem to the maître d' and ask if he could take the saucepans into the kitchen and ask the chef if it would be possible to put a little food into each, so that they looked as if they had been used. We would tell the customs, when asked if we had anything to declare, that we had found eating out in France so expensive that we had had to buy saucepans to cook for ourselves, and as they were used in France we would not have to pay duty on them when entering the UK.

The maître d' thought the whole idea very funny and was more than willing to help. I was told to go to the car and fetch the saucepans. The maître d' took the saucepans into the kitchen and brought them back stained with food. My father paid for the meal and we left the restaurant and drove to the ferry terminal, where we boarded the ferry.

Next morning, we drove off the boat and into what was then the customs shed. A customs officer was standing behind one of the old-fashioned high desks. He was a thin man with a narrow face and a pointed nose. He looked awful. His face was very pale and he appeared to be clenching his buttocks. Either he had a stomach complaint or he had had too much to drink the night before.

My mother was driving and told my terrified father, who was sitting next to her not to speak — she would handle everything. As my mother stopped by the officer he asked if we had anything to declare. My mother told him she had bought two hundred cigarettes on the boat and my father four ounces of tobacco (both the permissible maximum to bring into the country). Then she told him we had holidayed in France, which was a lie, and that we had found it so expensive to eat out that she had bought saucepans and cooked for us. With that the customs officer said, "Is that all?" Mother replied, "yes," and he waved us through. Driving out of the port, my father heaved a great sigh of relief and we arrived home several hours later.

Once home the saucepans were put to use but unfortunately were not a great success, because when knocked against another hard object or sharp edge the enamel chipped easily, so they soon became very unattractive. Within a few months my mother stopped using them and went back to using her old, grey aluminium pans.

Sometime in early autumn 1961 my mother began to feel unwell and also began to complain about us living in the converted prisoner-of-war hut and in Marbury itself. Also, at about the same time, the chemical company sold the Hall and some of the surrounding land (including my father's nursery) to a property developer.

My father became worried that the land, including the nursery, would be developed for housing and so he would lose his livelihood. A friend of his offered to sell him some land on which he could rebuild the nursery and a house. Although the idea of us living in a proper house appealed greatly to my mother it did not help her overcome her health problems, and eventually she was diagnosed as having to have a hysterectomy. She was told that she would only be (at the most) two weeks in hospital.

A few weeks before Christmas she was admitted into Warrington General Hospital and the operation was carried out quickly and successfully. Unfortunately, soon afterwards she got an infection, which became steadily worse. As a result, she nearly died and was probably saved through the use of antibiotics. She stayed in hospital over Christmas and finally came home in January 1962. She was still very weak and had to stay in bed for several weeks.

The operation caused her to be depressed and feel much weaker, so it took her nearly the rest of the year to fully recover. During this time my father realised the idea of moving his nursery business (including plants, greenhouses and heating systems) and having a house built was too great a financial and physical burden for him to undertake. My mother also came to realise that the whole project was beyond them.

The other problem was that in two years my father would be fifty and in six years so would my mother. They began to think of their old age, how long they would be able to keep doing the hard, physical nursery work, where they would live and ultimately how they would manage to live on basic old-age pensions. I showed very little interest in the nursery apart from helping out on the market on a Saturday, so they could not rely on me taking it over and making sufficient success to support them and myself.

During this time, they met a couple who were retired. He had been with the police in Liverpool and during the latter part of his career he had managed to purchase a large old Victorian house, which contained many rooms. He had converted the rooms into bed-sitting rooms and therefore had supplemented his police pension to enjoy a comfortable life.

My parents began to consider the idea and soon realised that this could be a way out of their concerns regarding their old age. They thought more and more about this idea and finally, in late 1962, they saw a large Victorian or Edwardian red brick semi-detached house in Hartford, Northwich, for sale. They scraped together the deposit and managed, with a mortgage, to buy the house. Fortunately, the lady selling the house was moving into a much smaller property and so my mother and father managed to negotiate that much of the furniture in the house would be included in the sale. This was very helpful in order to furnish the bed-sitting rooms and the extra living space we were to enjoy.

5 West Park Marbury, Northwich, Cheshire U.K. The bungalow as my
mother would call it.
Actually a converted P.o.W. hut,
which we lived in from 1955 to 1963

My mother in front of Bedford van, which my father bought because
the nursery business was becoming successful. Torbay, Devon, England
summer 1958

Around Bianca Blaschke's grave Peter, Helen, Henry, Christine Frank;
Hildegard, Brigitte, Jupp, Waldtraut Hagel & Adolf Blaschke Warburton summer 1959

The bedsitting room business, .Hartford, Northwich, Cheshire, England
1960s

Henry Frank with Skipper the Labrador in back garden Hartford, Northwich, Cheshire, England late 1960s

Henry and Christine Frank, Northwich Sailing Club, Winsford Flashes,
Winsford, Cheshire, England 1970

Henry and Christine Frank on their 40th wedding
anniversary with their grandchildren Vanessa and
Matthew July 1980

Chapter 13

Bedsits, Azaleas, Australia and the End of the Plant Nursery

Eventually in March 1963, after ten years in Marbury, we moved to Beech Road, Hartford. My father, with the help of some friends, built (in the four rooms he planned to rent out in the house) a kitchenette with a washing-up sink, and installed in each a gas cooker, gas fire and electricity and gas meters. The rooms were furnished with a table, a couple of chairs, a bed and a wardrobe from the items that had been included in the purchase of the house. Fortunately, there were two bathrooms so one was allocated to us as our family bathroom and the other to the tenants. Having completed all the alterations, my mother began to advertise for tenants and soon all four rooms were let.

Although there were many changes of tenants, one or two either remained with them for several years or returned. I distinctly remember one Brazilian couple. He had been sent from a chemical company in Brazil for a year's secondment to the local chemical factory. Towards the end of their stay they found a stray cat and amazingly persuaded my mother that they could keep it in their room. They took it back to Brazil when they returned and for many years afterwards always sent my parents a Christmas card picturing themselves, their growing family of children and the cat.

A year or two before, Northwich had agreed a twin-town arrangement with the French town Dole. Part of the arrangement was the ability for school children over the age of sixteen to have exchanges, so that French school students would come to Northwich for three weeks to improve their English and then vice versa. Having failed my French "O" Level exam at least twice my father hoped, by me being part of the programme, that I would improve my French to a point that I would pass the exam.

In mid-July a boy called Alain came to us and three weeks later I went with him to France. Of course, his English improved dramatically — so much so that when I went to France, we continued to speak English. I failed the French "O" Level exam six times in all, before I left school at eighteen.

In 1964 my parents sold the Allard and bought a Hillman Imp, which was the complete opposite of the Allard: small and light but still quite fast. My parents liked the Imp so much they bought three of them in succession. In early summer I failed all my "A" Levels and so ended my parents hope that I would go on to further education. Instead I got a job as a bonus clerk with the Ilford Film Company in Ilford (then in Essex and now part of East London). As a result, I moved away from home and memories of my parents become much less. I would go home perhaps once a month but only for a short weekend and when home would spend time with my friends and not much with my parents.

They went to Germany in summer 1965 to visit our relations in Hamburg and in 1967 they went to Austria, visiting St. Gilgen and Pernitz, where Evy von Semann lived at the time. They also went to Vienna. It was my father's first visit to Vienna since he left in May 1939. I remember him telling me he went into the bank where he had had an account in 1939 and asked if it was still open, but they said they had no record of him or his account.

About this time my father decided he needed another major crop to supplement his Cyclamen and Hydrangeas and decided to try growing Azaleas from cuttings. Azaleas originate from the Himalayas, where very young plants survive mainly from the mountain mist (as the ground drains very quickly because of the steep terrain). Being an avid horticulturist, he read everything available about propagating Azaleas in a glasshouse.

He knew that the soil should be of a very poor quality, which was no problem to create, but the cuttings would only thrive if the air around them remained very moist and cool like mountain mist. This did not mean watering them constantly because Azaleas like to stand in soil that drains easily. He discovered that a firm had invented an artificial electronic leaf that allowed moisture to collect on it and, once it began to dry beyond a certain point, would switch on a very fine spray to create the ideal mountain mist conditions for Azalea cuttings to grow successfully. He enquired about buying such a device and on learning the price realised he could not afford one.

He had a friend who often helped him at weekends in the nursery. Although not trained in the subject, this man had taught himself electronics. He suggested to my father that they try making such a device themselves. So, every weekend (usually on a Sunday) they would work on the project. His friend built the electronic circuitry and my father the propagating bench and the fine nozzles to create the mist conditions.

They created the leaf using aluminium foil attached to two electrodes. The foil was sprayed with water and as it dried out the resistance across the electrodes became greater to the point where it switched on the water to spray both the Azalea cuttings and the foil. Once the resistance reduced to the point at which the tin foil was again sufficiently wet, the electronics switched off the water spray. That was the theory, but it took a long time to create the electronic circuitry that was sufficiently sensitive to ensure that the cuttings were not completely flooded or dried out completely. After months of Sundays they began to get close to achieving their goal by continually modifying the circuitry.

Now I must explain three things. Firstly, the circuitry was mounted on a wooden board just above the propagating bench and was protected from the spray by a plastic cover. Secondly, the circuit diagram was drawn in chalk on the same wooden board and modified as they modified the actual circuitry. Thirdly, my father's friend had a very bad speech impediment.

Finally, one Sunday, they felt they had the circuitry sufficiently sensitive for it to operate properly. So, they sprayed the tin foil, switched on both the electronics and the water and waited for the foil to dry sufficiently. To expedite matters my father borrowed my mother's hair dryer to speed up the drying process.

Suddenly the water began to spray all over the cuttings and the tin foil. It all seemed to work perfectly, except they had forgotten to put the protective cover on the circuit board. Then my father's friend realised the danger. He tried to tell my father, who was standing closer to the switch for the electronics and the tap for the water, to shut down the system but unfortunately nothing came out of his mouth and my father, who was looking on in awe and amazement at what they had created, was not aware of the impending disaster.

The bare electronics became wet and shorted, with sparks and a bang. The chalk circuit diagram was completely washed away. My father then became aware of what had happened and swung into action, turning off the water then the power but all too late. All the electronic components were destroyed and they now had no circuit diagram from which to create another circuit board. Totally despondent and devastated they gave up.

Very soon after, the price of the system one could purchase dropped dramatically and my father immediately acquired one. He was one of the first nurserymen in the UK to grow azaleas commercially from cuttings and did so very successfully until he retired.

In late 1967 I moved back in with my parents. I now had a job with International Computers Ltd (ICL), travelling around the country on expenses and nearly all the time had to work overtime. I was earning a healthy income.

One weekend I was sitting at home feeling rather bored and thinking back to our sailing on Lake Geneva in the summer of 1961. I mentioned to my father that I would like to buy a sailing dinghy and learn to sail. He jumped at the idea and we looked in the local paper and there was a GP14 (General Purpose 14 foot) sailing dinghy for sale. We bought it that very day and immediately took up sailing on Winsford Flashes.

The flashes are small lakes formed when the bed of the River Weaver sank due to the underground brine extraction I mentioned earlier. After a few months we joined the Northwich Sailing Club and began racing every Sunday from late spring to early autumn. A couple of years later we bought another sailing dinghy, a new Albacore, and also raced it.

Sailing, especially dinghy sailing, can be a very wet sport. Being young I didn't mind getting wet but it caused rheumatism in my father's joints, so he bought a matching waterproof jacket and salopettes. When I saw him in them for the first time, I remarked that he must have a lot of money to buy such an outfit. He replied that they were not really for sailing, they were protective clothing to be used when he was spraying his crops. As usual with my father he claimed them as a business expense and was therefore able to offset the cost of them against his income tax. He never used them at the nursery because he did not spray his crops.

I came downstairs one morning to hear my father shouting and cursing, which was not unusual for him. On asking him what the problem was he replied that he had received an income tax demand. I asked how much tax the Inland Revenue were demanding. He said that it was for four pounds and ninety-four pence. I enquired if this was for the month, because I paid Pay As You Earn Income Tax. He panicked for a moment, looked at the demand again, regained his composure and said that, no, that this was for the year. Now I already paid much more than this per month so suggested that he had misread the sum and that it was more likely to be for four hundred and ninety four pounds. At this point he became white with fear and again checked the sum; to his utter relief it really was for four pounds ninety-four pence.

Absolutely exasperated with him I walked past, saying that he should stop complaining and pay up. Over breakfast he continued to be very upset, saying he had never paid income tax in all his time in business and that he paid an accountant to ensure he did not have to pay it. I went off to my job thinking: if only I could be so lucky as to pay such a small amount of tax.

On returning that evening I asked him what he intended to do about the demand. He explained he had spoken to his accountant and that the accountant said that he had managed to make an agreement with the Inland Revenue that this was the minimum sum the Inland Revenue would accept, and my father had to pay it. The accountant went on to tell my father that if he queried or contested the amount the Inland Revenue would do a complete audit of his business. At this point my father relented and agreed to pay but in a closing shot to the accountant said, "I pay you so that I don't pay any income tax, therefore I will deduct the four pounds ninety-four pence from your bill."

For some reason my parents never, to my knowledge, celebrated their twenty-fifth wedding anniversary in July 1965. However, in 1970 my mother was determined that they would celebrate their thirtieth. It was not a big affair. In fact, she booked a table for four at the Golden Pheasant in Plumley, a village near Northwich, summoning Helen, me and of course my father to attend. I remember little about the dinner but at least my mother was pleased that we as a family were together for the celebration — never mind how small it was, because none of our other relations lived in the UK.

In late 1973 I married and in summer of 1974 got a job with ICL's subsidiary in Sydney, Australia. My parents were both pleased and sad that my now ex-wife and I were going to Australia. Pleased because at the time the economic situation in the UK was very bleak and Australia was seen as the land of opportunity. Sad, because they were worried they would not see us again, or at best only very infrequently.

We were due to leave for Australia on 8th August 1974 and my parents had arranged to go on holiday a few days before we were due to leave, so my then wife and I took them to the station and said goodbye as we would be gone before they came back from holiday. This reminded my father of having never seen his parents again after he waved goodbye to them at West Station, Vienna, in May 1939. My mother had similar feelings because she only saw her mother twice after leaving Poland in January 1939 and her father only a few times more. But we went with their blessings, as they both thought it was the best for us.

My wife and I arrived in Sydney a few days later, having had a stop off in Singapore. In April 1975 our son was born; he gave us great pleasure and in late 1975 my parents wrote to say they were coming to visit us for six weeks in Sydney, having bought cheap return tickets. They left England in mid-February.

The cheap tickets meant they would fly to Delhi, where they would change planes, arriving some thirty hours later in Sydney. Having stocked up with extra food and prepared all sorts of treats for my parents we, with our ten-month-old son one Sunday morning, drove off to Sydney airport to meet them. On enquiring at the information desk if the flight from Delhi was on time, we were told there was no such flight due to arrive that day or any other day, because the flight number did not exist. We returned home utterly dejected and none the wiser as to what had happened to them.

My parents told us later that unfortunately when they landed in Delhi, they were told their tickets were not valid for a connecting flight to Sydney, and they would have to pay full price for the onward flight. Fortunately, there were a number of people who had bought similar tickets from London to Australia. They quickly formed an action group and after much complaining to the airline manager at Delhi airport he agreed to provide taxis for them to the headquarters building in Delhi.

There they invaded the chief executive officer's outer office with their luggage and settled down for a long siege. The CEO soon realised it did not look good having these people in his outer office and worried about the poor publicity that the action group were threatening, so he put them into one of Delhi's best hotels (all expenses paid) until the problem could be resolved.

After four days the Delhi airport station manager came to see them saying the problem had been resolved: they would have to fly via Hong Kong, stay overnight at the airline's expense and then fly on to Sydney with another airline the next day. A day later they boarded the flight to Hong Kong. On landing there, and having been once bitten, they immediately checked on the next day's flight to Sydney. This time they were told it was full and so were all subsequent flights.

Once again, they harangued the airline's airport manager; he arranged and paid for taxis to take them to where the general manager had his office in the heart of Hong Kong; the office was fortunately not far from the hotel into which they were booked. As in Delhi, they again invaded the general manager's office and to placate them he said the airline would pay their hotel expenses until suitable flights could be found.

There was a problem at the Hong Kong airport at that time that was restricting the number of take-offs and landings, and consequently causing a huge backlog of passengers. One very sad story my parents told me, when they finally arrived in Sydney, was of an Australian couple who were on holiday in Hong Kong and while there, their son had been killed in car accident. They immediately wanted to cut short their stay in Hong Kong and return home but could not get a flight. In the end, pressure from the Australian High Commission managed to get them on a flight some days later.

For my parents, having had five days all expenses paid in Delhi and now the same in Hong Kong, it was very different matter: they thoroughly enjoyed themselves. Every day the whole action group met in the general manager's office to ensure they were not forgotten. After five days the airline finally managed to get them on a flight to Sydney. The first we knew about it was at about 8.00 a.m. one morning when my parents called us to say they had finally arrived at Sydney airport. They took a taxi and we saw them for the first time since we left England some twenty months earlier.

As a result of their lengthy stopovers in Delhi and Hong Kong, their stay with us was foreshortened by nearly two weeks. However, in that time we managed to take them to the Gold Coast and Brisbane, driving there on the then Pacific Highway. We returned to Sydney by the inland route via New England and Armadale. A few days later we took them to Canberra and down to the south coast of New South Wales via the Snowy Mountains. We also took them on local trips in and around Sydney and on the Captain Cook's tour boat trip of Sydney harbour.

Fortunately, their return trip to England went off without a problem. For them Australia was a trip of a lifetime, which they never forgot. They wanted us to stay because they were so impressed by the country, the people, the food and the weather. Fortunately for them they had missed the weather in January when it rained for eight days nonstop and all our leather clothes and shoes were covered in mould.

In October 1976, just two years and three months after we arrived in Australia, we decided to return to the UK, for the following reasons. My wife was pregnant with our second child and we wanted our children to know their grandparents (unlike me, who only very vaguely remembered my maternal grandmother and only saw my maternal grandfather four times, and could never communicate with him). On moving back to the UK my firm gave me a sales job in Edinburgh, where in June 1977 our daughter was born, giving us even more pleasure in knowing we now had a complete family.

In late 1976 my parents bought a tent and used it a couple times on European holidays. In the spring of 1977, they took it to Spain, where the weather was already sufficiently warm to enjoy camping. Their campsite was near the beach and the sea was warm enough to swim every day.

The most amazing coincidence occurred while they were camping in France during the summer of 1977. In the neighbouring tent was an Australian family on a European touring holiday. They got talking with them, explaining that they had been in Australia in 1976. The Australians asked where they had stayed and my parents gave them our then address in Willoughby, a suburb of North Sydney. The man expressed surprise, saying that he was a jobbing builder and had done work in the house where my parents had stayed with us in Australia.

In early summer they returned from Spain full of the joys of camping. By this time, it was becoming more difficult to find tenants for their bed-sitting rooms. People were becoming better off and hence rented flats or houses or were able to buy their own properties. They realised the big house was going to be costly to maintain and heat without the income from tenants.

At the same time a friend of theirs was selling a town house nearby. They enquired at the local estate agents about what they could expect for their current house and were very pleasantly surprised at how much it had appreciated over the fifteen years they had lived there. So much so they were able to sell it and buy the town house outright, pay off the outstanding amount on the mortgage and still have a significant capital sum to invest to support them in their old age.

So, in late summer 1977 they moved about a mile along Beech Road. At about the same time they gave up the nursery because it was becoming too hard for them. A young man had come to work for my father a year or so earlier. He was a very keen horticulturist who loved working in the nursery. My father approached him as to whether he would be keen on taking over the business. He jumped at the chance. Because the property was rented and the greenhouses, heating systems and other equipment were quite old, my father sold him the business at a price the man could afford. So, after twenty-four years of having his own businesses my father happily finished with the nursery and the bed-sitting rooms.

Chapter 14

The Final Years

Later, in 1977, my parents decided they wanted to again go to Spain camping. They planned to drive through France, taking a detour to Switzerland to visit Uncle Herbert's widow Mary in Geneva. Herbert had died in 1973. About two-thirds of the way through France they stopped for petrol. The petrol pumps were mounted on a raised concrete platform. My father got out to unlock the petrol cap. He did not see that oil had been spilled on the ground where he was about to walk. Suddenly he slipped sideways, falling on to the raised concrete platform, with his left hip hitting the edge. He felt a very sharp pain and realised he could not stand up. The owner immediately called an ambulance and he was taken to hospital with my mother following in the car.

In hospital he was quickly diagnosed as having a broken hip. He had an operation and was in hospital for three weeks. My mother stayed in a bed-and-breakfast nearby. Fortunately, he had full travel insurance, so everything was covered. Eventually, once he had recovered sufficiently, they said he could go home, but he still could not walk or drive. The insurance company decided that he would have to be flown home with my mother, and the car would be transported home separately.

Once home, my father set about claiming compensation from the petrol station's insurance company. The local hospital in Northwich X-rayed his hip and declared that the operation had been performed to a very high standard.

It took over six weeks for the car to be returned to my parents because the car transporter had broken down somewhere on an Alpine pass in the middle of winter. The driver had no warm clothing so he took what he needed from the various cars on the transporter to keep warm. In my parents' case he stole a sleeping bag and a pair of my father's underpants.

By spring 1978 my father had recovered but from then on always walked with a limp, and often had to resort to a walking stick. My parents decided that their camping days were over so instead bought a small caravan, which in autumn they took to Spain for several weeks.

Again, they enjoyed the warmth, being near a beach, swimming in the sea and, above all, the low cost of living, which was then available in Spain. In addition, they saved on heating costs in their house in England and living in a caravan for several weeks was much more comfortable than in a tent.

With this in mind, they began to think of moving to Spain — not permanently but at least for each winter. As well as the reasons above, my mother suffered badly from angina pectoris. The cold winter winds of England could easily bring on an attack at any time, whereas the attacks did not occur with anything like the same frequency in the warmth of a Spanish winter. But they simply could not afford the capital to buy a place.

In summer 1978 my parents were in London visiting my sister and her husband when, by chance, they met an Austrian couple who lived in London and were of a similar age to my parents. They got into conversation and they explained that, like my father, they were of Jewish origin and were forced to leave Austria before the beginning of the war. Suddenly the couple asked if my father was receiving his war crimes pension from the Austrian government. My father was surprised to hear that such a thing existed. They explained how one could apply for it through a lawyer in Vienna, provided one had documentation to prove one was born in Austria and had been forced to leave in order to escape persecution.

Fortunately, my father had kept all his Austrian documents — particularly those declaring that he had been classified as a Jew. The couple gave my father the name and address of the lawyer, and my father contacted him. Having sent him copies of all relevant documents, several months later my father was informed that he would receive a small pension from the Austrian Government's war crimes fund. This supplemented his income and helped my mother and father to enjoy the last few years of their lives.

Interestingly, when my father died it was thought that the pension would die with him. However, when my mother wrote to the appropriate department in Austria to say that her husband had died, they replied stating that she was eligible to receive half of his pension until her death, provided she could provide a birth certificate, marriage certificate and proof of where she had lived during her life. The problem was that my mother did not take her birth certificate with her when she left Poland, and her parents left it behind when they fled from the Russians. She had proof of her life in Britain after arriving in 1939 through her Aliens' Registration Certificate, Naturalisation Documents and British Passport, but could not think how to prove she was born in what became Poland.

One day while in my office I received a telephone call from her asking if I could help in any way. She sounded very distressed at the possibility of losing her half of the Austrian pension. I explained that she had once told me she still had her original Polish Identity Document and Passport plus the return train ticket to Poland that she was never able to use. I suggested that if she could find them, she should take all of the above, plus the British documents, to the family solicitor (who was a Notary Public) and get him to make notarised copies of everything and then send them to Austria with an explanatory letter. This she did, and as a result she received the reduced pension until her death. It just shows how important it is to retain all personal documents throughout one's life.

In early 1979 the French petrol station's insurance company agreed to pay compensation of about five thousand pounds. At that time the French Franc was worth less than the English Pound. So instead of having the funds transferred to his English bank account my father asked the insurance company if they would hold the money in French Francs until he was able to decide what to do with it. The French insurance company was more than happy to do this.

In spring 1979 my parents again took the caravan down to Spain. While driving through Benalmadina they saw a placard offering cheap studio apartments for sale. They enquired and discovered that an apartment hotel called Hotel Playa Sol was offering to sell studio apartments on the following basis: the purchase was one million pesetas (about five thousand pounds) for the use of the apartment from mid-October to mid-March; the hotel would pay all council taxes and electricity bills, and redecorate the apartment each year in early October; the hotel would have the use of the apartment to let to holidaymakers from the beginning of April to the end of September. My parents jumped at the chance and bought one using the insurance money in France.

They used it for the first time in autumn 1979, staying until March 1980. They drove from Cheshire to Plymouth, where they caught the car ferry to Santander in northern Spain. The journey took about 24 hours, so my parents regarded it as a mini-sea-cruise. They then drove right through Spain, north to south, to Benalmadina, where they stayed in their studio apartment until March.

They returned to England via Geneva, where they visited Herbert's widow Mary. From Geneva they drove on to Freiburg to visit an old school friend of my mother from Upper Silesia. Then they went to Austria to visit Evy Seemann, and finally to Hamburg to see my mother's sister Waldtraut and her husband Jupp. From Hamburg they took the ferry to Harwich in England and then drove home to Cheshire. They did this five times from October 1979 to March 1983.

They loved their time in Spain, especially the warmth and sunshine. The beach was just across the road so my father, especially, went swimming nearly every day; my mother just loved to sit in the sun. The apartment had two balconies, one on the east side and the other on the west side of the building. The hotel was built so that it pointed more or less due north and south.

After breakfast my father would go to the beach and often my mother would sit on the east balcony in the sun. From about 11.30 a.m. the sun would begin to shine on the south end of the hotel so my mother would go into the flat and prepare lunch, and my father would return from the beach. After lunch, my father would return to the beach and my mother would sit on the west balcony until about 5.00 p.m., when the sun began to go down. She would then prepare the evening meal and my father would return from the beach.

This routine was only broken when they had to go shopping, meet with friends or went sightseeing. As in Britain, they made many friends in Spain — mainly other migratory English ex-pats — and spent many happy hours with them.

However, there was one exception. As they always stayed in Spain over Christmas they had agreed to meet up with a group of these friends for an evening. They had just got ready to go when the wife from one of the English couples in the group rang to say that my parents were not welcome to join the group that evening. On asking why, she said that her husband was not happy to have a Jew such as Henry in their midst at Christmas. My father had probably explained to them and the others about how and why he had had to leave Austria in May 1939, but perhaps not explained that he was, and had always been, a Christian. As a result, my parents were very disappointed at being left out and made other arrangements to enjoy the evening by themselves.

I think my father was, to say the least, more than disappointed, thinking that after a period of over forty years living in a tolerant country (that had saved him from the Holocaust and accepted him fully into its society) anti-Semitism should come back to haunt him in his last years.

A day or so later they met some of the rest of the group with whom they should have enjoyed the evening. They asked why Henry and Christine had not joined them. The offending couple were not present and so my parents explained what had happened, and also that my father had been christened and had remained a Christian all his life. The group were horrified and especially embarrassed by what the offending couple had done, so much so that they told the couple what they thought of them and explained Henry's religious position to them. They insisted that the man publicly apologise to my parents in their midst.

One other event worthy of mention occurred because, at that time, Spain was not in the European Union — so my parents were only allowed to remain in the country for a maximum of three months at a time. So, they would drive to Portugal for a couple of nights and then return to Benalmadina.

On one such occasion my parents decided to accompany another English couple in their car. During the journey, a motorbike with a pillion passenger appeared to overtake and when parallel and close to the car the pillion rider smashed the front passenger window with a hammer. My parents were sitting in the rear seat and because it was a right-hand drive car driving on the right-hand side of the road, the pillion passenger was able to reach into the car and snatch the handbag from the lap of the wife of my parents' friends. The motorbike then drove off at speed. Naturally the driver of the car stopped to check his wife was not injured, and then they drove on and in the next town reported the incident to the police.

In early 1980 my family and I moved from Edinburgh, Scotland, to a village on the west side of Coventry, England. In March a woman came to the door saying that in 1981 a national census would be carried out. She explained that they had designed the forms, which were to be completed by each household, and asked if I was prepared to complete what was then the draft form. I agreed and she gave me instructions as to how to complete it. She explained that apart from entering my name and address I had to enter the name, nationality and country of birth of everybody who stayed overnight on the following Sunday to Monday. She told me she would collect the completed forms on the Tuesday and return a few days later to ask me if I had found any difficulties in completing the form.

It just so happened that my parents returned from Spain that weekend and stayed with us over the Sunday night. So, I dutifully completed the form on the Monday evening as follows: name Peter Frank, nationality British, country of birth Wales; Irene Frank, nationality British, country of birth England; Matthew Frank, nationality British, country of birth Australia; Vanessa Frank, nationality British, country of birth Scotland; Henry Frank, British, country of birth Austria; Christine Frank, nationality British, country of birth Poland (please note that I did not know at that time that my mother had actually been born in the former German Empire).

The lady collected the form the next day and a few days later returned, ostensibly to discuss any problems I had had completing it. She began by asking if I thought the whole exercise was a joke? I asked her to explain what she meant. She said, "Well, every person you say stayed in this house last Sunday night was born in a different country — surely this cannot be true." I assured her that it was the case. She laughed and enquired if I had had any difficulties completing the form, to which I replied that I hadn't, and she left — still chuckling to herself.

In July 1980 my mother and father celebrated their fortieth wedding anniversary. Again, it was a small affair but larger than their thirtieth. This time, Helen was married and her husband Albert was present. My former wife and I had our son and daughter, Matthew and Vanessa, with us. We were all invited to a lunch at the Rheingold Restaurant in yet another village near Northwich. It was owned and run by the woman who had accompanied my mother in 1955 on the journey to Germany and back.

We had a sumptuous meal and then returned to my parents' house, where my mother said that she had prepared a light afternoon tea "for anyone who still felt a bit peckish". We all said that we had eaten our fill but would welcome a cup of tea. My mother immediately disappeared into the kitchen. We sat in the lounge, talking with my father and playing with our children. After a while my father called to my mother saying, "Chris, what is taking you so long to make a pot of tea?"

A couple of minutes later my mother replied, "Come through to the dining room, it is on the dining table." Thinking that there would be just teacups, milk, sugar and a pot of tea there, we all went into the dining room. What we found was a banquet of cold food, including a whole cold cooked salmon, plates of various cold meats, sandwiches, salads, a bowl of her signature chocolate mousse, a large cake and other sundry items.

We were all overwhelmed and sadly had to disappoint my mother, saying we had all eaten our fill at the restaurant and now just wanted a cup of tea. My father asked her why she had gone to so much trouble on their wedding anniversary. My mother replied, "Well, I thought you would all have appreciated a little snack after the meal." I don't know what happened to all the food. My former wife and I left soon after with our children to drive back to Coventry. Helen and Albert returned by train to London that evening.

During one period in Spain my father bought an inflatable sailing dinghy, which he loved to sail on the sea. In March 1983 he was sailing to the shore when a large wave capsized the dinghy in shallow water. My father fell into the sea and landed hard on the seabed. He recovered from the initial shock and pulled the dinghy on to the beach, where he rested for a while before deflating it. He then carried it back to the apartment. It took him a few days to fully recover from the shock and bruising, during which time he didn't sail. Then it was time to pack up and begin the long journey from southern Spain, via northern Germany, to England.

Once home he appeared to have fully recovered but then he started to experience pains in his stomach and was diagnosed with a stomach ulcer, for which he received medicine and this appeared to remedy the problem. In May my mother and father took the caravan to their favourite caravan site in Wales; the weather was glorious and they thoroughly enjoyed their time there.

On returning, my father began to experience pains in various joints and bones of his body. The doctor diagnosed this as arthritis and prescribed him painkillers, but the pains became worse — to the point that he could hardly walk. My mother took him to a specialist, who confirmed the GPs diagnosis.

On the last Sunday in late July my wife and children and I went to visit my parents. My father was sitting in an upright chair, because by now he could no longer sit in armchair or on a sofa. I was alone in the lounge with him when he said, "Peter, it is time for us to have a last talk." I could not believe he was about to die and thought he was just being dramatic, so I replied, "Don't be silly, you are not about to die — we have lots of time for that last talk."

As the pains increased, I recommended that my mother take him to another specialist for a second opinion. The second specialist took one look at him and recommended that he be admitted into hospital. My father had been in the Free Masons since the early 1960s and asked the specialist to refer him to the Free Masons Hospital in West London. A friend of my father took him and my mother to London, where my father was admitted to the hospital. My mother stayed with my sister in her and her husband's flat, and visited my father every day.

My wife and I, and our children, went to visit him the following weekend. On seeing him I could see he had lost a lot of weight and they were already sedating him heavily. I was very concerned for him. I left the ward and found a doctor, who happened to be the consultant responsible for my father. The consultant explained that on X-raying him they had found that he had bone cancer and he gave my father only a few weeks to live.

The hospital tried to slow the bone cancer by giving him radiotherapy treatment, but to no avail. My mother, sister, brother in-law and I visited for the last time on Saturday 3rd September, but by then he was being heavily sedated with morphine so I never had that last chance to talk with him. He died on Sunday 4th September 1983.

My mother called me on the Sunday morning to say dad had died. She was heartbroken. She had met him in October 1939 and they were married in July 1940. She had known him for 44 years and had been married to him for 43 of them. They had celebrated their fortieth wedding anniversary in 1980.

They had struggled through the war, not knowing what would happen to them. Then a few years later they struggled to build a nursery business and later a bedsit business. Only in the last few years did they have the comfort of a proper home, completely to themselves, and the opportunity to enjoy pleasant warm winters in Spain.

On Tuesday 6th September I drove to London and took my mother and Helen back to Cheshire. Funeral arrangements were made, including bringing my father's body back to be cremated at Dunham Massey Crematorium the following week.

After the funeral my mother settled down to life on her own. She went to see her sister Waldtraut in Hamburg and spent Christmas with us in Coventry. The next year she visited Mary in Geneva and Evy Seemann in Wiener-Neustadt in Austria. She went back to the flat in Spain. She sold the caravan but naturally kept the car.

She had several friends in Northwich and kept up a lively social life. In 1985 she sold the flat in Spain (back to the hotel) and boasted to our children that she was now a millionaire, but only a Spanish peseta millionaire. In the winter of 1985—1986 she rented a flat in Spain for a few weeks before returning to Northwich in March.

Soon after she returned, I telephoned her to ask how she was and she said that she was not well — with aches all over her body. She went to the doctor, who diagnosed rheumatoid arthritis. He prescribed painkillers but they didn't seem to help. She heard from a friend who had also suffered from the same complaint that a course of steroids would cure her.

So, she went to the doctor and asked him to prescribe them. He was reluctant to do so because of my mother's angina pectoris, but my mother insisted. The doctor relented, saying that if they caused stress on her heart then she should stop taking them by slowly reducing the dose.

The dose consisted of three large disc-like tablets the size of small coffee cup saucers, taken three times a day, that had to be dissolved in water. After each dose she had to lie down because of the stress on her heart. After a week she felt terrible and told me she that she had stopped taking them. I reminded her that she must not stop taking them so suddenly, but she said that she was feeling much better.

On Thursday 12th June I had to go to Manchester for a meeting and on my way home I called in to see her. She appeared amazingly well and in very good spirits, saying that when she was fully recovered she would start travelling again by going to see her sister in Hamburg. I left her, thinking that she was on the road to recovery.

On Friday I telephoned to see how she was and she told me she felt a little tired, but that was all. She felt an early night was all she needed. On Saturday I telephoned and she said she still felt tired, and that some of her aches and pains were returning. She said the same on Sunday, so I told her to call the doctor on Monday and make an appointment to see him.

On Monday I had to fly to Edinburgh for a meeting so I left early and only returned home around 9.00 pm. I phoned her. She said she was feeling very unwell and began to cry. She explained that she had not called the doctor because she was too tired to do so. She went on to say that she wanted to see the Black Madonna of Cestahova in Poland and wanted some good Polish black bread. I was shocked at how nostalgic she was but after a few minutes she seemed to recover, and I promised to call her the next day.

As I was leaving for the office on Tuesday morning my sister called to say that a neighbour had called her to say our mother was not well, and that she had called an ambulance. I called my mother to ask what was wrong and she said she was feeling very unwell; before I could speak again, she said, "Peter, I can't talk anymore…!" The phone went dead and I was left shouting down the phone, asking my mother if she was all right. I received no answer.

I put the phone down and a few minutes later Helen called to say that the neighbour had been back in to see my mother. She was lying in bed and appeared to be sleeping; could I go immediately to Northwich?

My wife suggested that I take an overnight bag, which I did, and drove to my mother's house.

In those days there weren't any car phones, let alone mobile phones, so no one could contact me until I arrived. On reaching the house I saw a police car parked outside. As I got out of the car, the neighbour who had tried to help my mother stood at the door, crying, and told me that my mother had died a couple of hours before. About the time she said to me "Peter, I can't talk anymore…!" I was the last one to speak to her. She may have died just after uttering those words!

I walked into the house and there was the policeman who asked me to formally identify the body, which I did. He gave his condolences and left. The neighbour went back to her house and I was left alone. My sister, who had got the next train from London, arrived a couple of hours later and we started to inform our immediate families, our mother's friends and our relations in Europe. I called the undertaker who had attended to our father in 1983. The funeral took place a week later at the same place where our father had been cremated.

The End